# ORGANISED FUN

## For Grown-Ups

# About the Author

Josie Curran is thirty-three years old and lives in a houseboat on an island in the Thames with her boyfriend, Barney, their dog and a gathering of adopted wildfowl. When she's not mucking about on beaches, campsites or under dinner tables, Josie works for Kids Company, assisting Camila Batmanghelidjh in her work with underprivileged children. She is the author of *Organised Fun: A treasure trove of games and tomfoolery* and *Organised Fun For Kids*.

# ORGANISED FUN

## For Grown-Ups

*Make your own fun for free*

Josie Curran

BⓍXTREE

First published 2009 by Boxtree
an imprint of Pan Macmillan Ltd

This edition published 2013 by Pan Books
an imprint of Pan Macmillan, a division of Macmillan Publishers Limited
Pan Macmillan, 20 New Wharf Road, London N1 9RR
Basingstoke and Oxford
Associated companies throughout the world
www.panmacmillan.com

ISBN 978-1-4472-6272-5

Designed and typeset by Ben Cracknell Studios

*To Barnaby Girling,
a feat of God's creating*

# Contents

# Introduction

We've all been there: at a dinner party or during an afternoon at the pub when conversation runs dry. It's not to say our friends and family are dull; it's just that sometimes exploring the meaning of life or discussing the finer details of your new mortgage agreement isn't the antidote we all need after a stressful week at work. But ideally within  every group there exists a Tigger-like character, someone who can be relied upon to bound forwards and introduce a game, guiding the gathering onwards to an escapade of fun.

I've always been that slightly annoying person, haranguing people incessantly until they cave in and join me in an afternoon or evening of play. From a civilised game of Fruit Croquet on the lawn to a session of Dune Jumping, I'm an ardent believer in the wholesome healing properties that make-your-own fun can provide.

Recent years have seen a resurgence of interest in homespun fun, from the feel-good anarchy in evidence at the explosion of festivals and flash-mob events to the erudite and often downright daft games that are gracing the sofas and dinner-party tables of society today. Permission has been granted for us to nurture our inner kidult. Teenage playfulness can last beyond the traditional age of eighteen, with many of us gambolling into our thirties, forties, fifties and beyond.

But it's not only the change in attitudes to permissible adult behaviour that is driving this zeitgeist. One reaction to the bling culture that pervaded the nineties and early noughties and the resulting global economic crash has been a reversion to traditional ways of living. This return to simpler values is seeing us reaching for the garden spade, darning our socks and coming up with ways to entertain ourselves that neither rely on technical advances nor, more importantly, cost us a penny. This positive response to the wider doom and gloom is creating an awareness of the bonding, binding beauty that organised fun can provide. Thrifty homespun fun is the movement of the moment and, thankfully, it looks here to stay for the foreseeable future.

# About This Book

*Organised Fun for Grown-Ups is packed full of inspiration for homespun fun and tomfoolery that will have you and your friends roaring with laughter in no time. Whether you're looking to impress, seduce or merely prevent an evening from becoming a bit tedious, you will find an abundance of novel ideas here that will earn you a bucketload of Brownie (or Cub Scout) points and guarantee you a place at the top of any dinner-party guest list.*

*The book is structured in such a way that wherever you are and whatever you're up to, you should easily find your way to a wealth of ideas for fun. I hope you find the book as pleasurable to read as the games are to play.*

# ONE

# Organised Fun for the Bar and Pub

Many a moon ago, you could be guaranteed an
evening of entertainment if you toddled down to
your local pub. Whether this was because people
hadn't quite developed the art of conversation
or simply because older generations had a more
natural aptitude for organised fun, I'm not sure.
Either way, you could be assured that from Darts
to Skittles and from Shove Ha'penny to Quoits,
your local boozer would offer a plethora of bar-
gaming delights. These days, as giant screens and
arcade games jostle for bar-side breathing space,
much is being written about the near-death of
traditional pub games.

Whether you're keen to keep such traditions
alive or merely looking for some bar-side fun, the
following chapter features some modern-day takes
on traditional games, alongside some novel ideas for
employing bar-based paraphernalia to keep you and
your beer buddies smiling well into the evening.

# Beer Mat Quoits

## What's the game?

Quoits is a traditional English pub game, which basically involves players lobbing a ring over a set of wooden stakes. The following adaptation can be easily rolled out at your local pub.

## What do I need to play it?

An orange or grapefruit, a cocktail stick and enough beer mats so that each player has two each.

## How many friends?

Between two and ten bar buddies is ideal.

## How do I play it?

- First of all, you need to prepare your equipment. Cut your orange or grapefruit in half, position one half flat side down on the table, and stick a cocktail stick in the middle of it.
- Next, create large, equal-sized holes in each of your beer mats. The smaller you make them, the harder the game.
- Distribute your beer mats so that each player has two, and mark a throwing line on the ground at an agreed distance away from the table, depending on how hard you want to make the game.
- In each round, players attempt to throw their two beer mats over the cocktail stick. If they get a 'hook' (i.e. get the mat hooked over the cocktail stick), the player scores three points; if it's a 'leaner' (if it leans against the cocktail stick), they get two points; if no one gets a hook or a leaner, then the person with the closest lob at the end of each round scores a point.
- The game plays on in the same way until someone reaches 21 points and they're declared the winner.

# Shove Ha'penny

## What's the game?

Shove Ha'penny is a vintage English classic invented by trainee lawyers in 1521. It is a smaller and more versatile adaptation of Shovel Board, which by all accounts was one of Henry VIII's favourite pastimes.

Shove Ha'penny has been a hugely popular pub game at local taverns for many a hundred year and it should do a marvellous job of keeping you entertained of an evening at your local brew house.

## What do I need to play it?

Some chalk, a bar or table to play on, permission from the barman to chalk on their table (it does wipe off, after all) and five of the same type of coins.

## How many friends?

Designed for two players, though you can create a tournament-style event if there are a few more of you.

## How do I play it?

- The traditional game is played using a Shove Ha'penny board, but as these are hard to come by at your local pub, you can draw your own board on the table or bar. To do this, simply chalk out ten lines, making sure that the distance between your lines is about one-and-a-half times the width of a coin. Next, mark out your shoving line about thirty centimetres in front of the first line.

- Each player takes it in turn to shove their five coins, aiming to get as many of them as possible to sit squarely in a bed – the gap between each of the horizontal lines. The coins must be positioned on the shoving line, and for each one that successfully lands in a bed, a chalk mark must be made by the side of the bed, with one player's marks made on one side and the other player's on the opposite side. A coin may be shoved only once, unless it doesn't reach the first line, in which case it can then be shoved again.

- Once a player has shoved all five of their coins, it's then the second player's turn to do the same.

- The aim is to get three chalk marks alongside each of the beds. However, once three scores have been made in a bed, any further scores in that bed will be given to the opponent instead, unless the opponent also has three scores in the bed.

- If your coin does land in a bed that's already scored three points, then you can try to knock it into the next one with one of your remaining coins.

- The first person to secure three points in each of their beds wins.

# Aunt Sally

## What's the game?

Aunt Sally is another traditional English pub game. Players must try to knock a doll off its perch. Traditionally, a wide iron stake was bashed into the ground and a wooden object was balanced on top which players would then attempt to knock off. Its roots lie in the English Civil War, when bored troops used to while away the hours between battles by knocking objects off posts.

In case you don't have an iron stake to hand, I've featured a pub-friendly version below.

## What do I need to play it?

A bar stool, three pieces of round fruit and some sort of non-smashing object that can be balanced and knocked off the stool (a light piece of wood is ideal).

## How many friends?

As many as are gathered around the bar.

## How do I play it?

- Each player has six tries at knocking the wooden item off the bar stool using the piece of fruit. Only underarm throws are allowed. There is no traditional rule on how far away from the stool you should stand, so just make your own rules based on the space available to you.

- The scores are totted up, and the person with the highest number of successful knock-offs wins that round and scores a point.

- The game plays through five rounds and the person with the highest number of points overall wins. If it's a draw, play moves into sudden death, with each player taking it in turns to attempt to knock the wooden block off the stool.

# Water Bottle Skittles

## What's the game?

Skittles has been found to date back to the seventeenth century and its journey through time is recorded in some famous works of literature. It was mentioned by Charles Dickens in *The Pickwick Papers* and even earlier by Thomas Hughes in *Tom Brown's Schooldays*. Because of the amount of bar space a traditional skittle alley takes up, the game is on the decline. Get behind the campaign to keep this classic game alive by bringing this easy-to-implement reinvention to a pub near you.

## What do I need to play it?

Ten recycled water bottles filled with water (you can decide which size you use, depending on the arm strength of your gathered players) and three grapefruits or cricket balls per player to be used as the bowling ball.

## How many friends?

Ideal for a small group of around six.

## How do I play it?

- Position your ten water bottles in a triangle and mark out a bowling distance about ten metres away. Get everyone into pairs.
- Each player takes it in turns to have three bowls to knock down as many water bottles as they can.
- At the end of each round, two points are awarded to the pair who knock down the most skittles. The game plays on until six rounds are completed.
- The team with the highest score wins.

# Cocktail-Stirrer Catapult Darts

## What's the game?

Cocktail-stirrers, as long as they're flexible enough, make great catapults. This game requires friendly bar staff who don't mind you flinging fruit slices onto the floor.

## What do I need to play it?

A cocktail-stirrer and three slices of lemon per player, and some chalk to mark out the dartboard.

## How many friends?

Ideal for two to four.

## How do I play it?

- Chalk out your dartboard on the floor. You can go to town and draw up the whole all-singing-and-dancing dartboard if you like; alternatively just draw three concentric circles with a bull's-eye in the middle. You'll also need to draw a flicking line for players to stand behind.

- Finally, agree your points system. You can either follow the rules of darts or make up your own, e.g. five points for a bull's-eye and then lower points for each of the wider circles.

- Players stand behind the flicking line with their slice of lemon positioned on the round flat top part of their cocktail-stirrer and then flick it towards the chalked dartboard on the floor.

- Points are totted up at the end of each round, with the winner being the highest-scoring player when play comes to an end.

# Coin Curling

## What's the game?

While away a rainy afternoon at the pub by flicking a bunch of coins towards a chalked-out target. The loser of each game has to buy the next round.

## What do I need to play it?

You need two coins of the same size and type per player and some chalk to mark out your target.

## How many friends?

However many are around to play, though any more than eight of you and it might mean too much waiting around.

## How do I play it?

- First of all, find yourself a lovely long table – the longer the better.
- Next, use the chalk to draw three circles of slowly decreasing size at one end of the table, each one inside the other, to form a target. Issue all players with two coins each, ensuring they are the same type to prevent calls of foul play.
- The aim of the game is to get your coins as near to the centre of the target as possible. You do this by standing at one end of the table and propelling your coin down to the other end with a flicking motion.
- Get yourselves into two teams. Players from each team take it in turns to flick both their coins towards the target.
- Once all players have played their turn, the winner is the team who got their coin closest to the smallest circle in the middle. One point is awarded for the coin closest to the centre and an additional point is awarded for all the winning team's coins that end up nearer the target than the loser's closest coin.
- The coins are collected, the game starts again and the first team to score twenty points wins.

# The Nail Game

## What's the game?

This is an Alpine classic, well known to anyone who's been on an Austrian skiing holiday and visited the local tavern. It's a test of judgement and strength in which players compete to be the one to hammer a nail all the way into a log. It provides a great opportunity for male bonding, as it combines strength, hammer dexterity and a healthy dose of competition in one neat 'hanging out at the bar' package.

## What do I need to play it?

A log, a hammer and some four-to-six-inch nails.

## How many friends?

I wouldn't recommend playing it with more than eight of you, as it could mean too much waiting around.

## How do I play it?

- The object of the game is to be the person who takes the final strike that gets the nail into the log.

- First, tap a good-sized nail a little way into a solid log or wooden block.

- Each player takes the hammer and strikes the nail in turn. If they are particularly bold, they might go for getting the nail all the way in. I've never seen anyone pull this off, though I am sure that if you're a challenger for the Austrian Championship it's a possibility.

- If, as is usually the case, the player only gets the nail a short way in, the hammer is handed around the group, with the striker to get the nail all the way in being declared the winner.

# Table Rugby

## What's the game?

This will appeal to rugby enthusiasts. It's kept us entertained for hours on many a rainy afternoon.

## What do I need to play it?

A table, a coin and two chairs.

## How many friends?

At least two of you.

## How do I play it?

- First up, players need to take it in turns to score a 'try'. A try is scored when a player successfully flicks a coin (using your index finger and thumb) to the other side of the table so that it lays flat and a part of it hangs over the edge.
- Players get three flick attempts; if they fail, it's the next player's turn. If successful, they then need to flick the coin off the edge of the table using index finger and thumb, and catch it as it falls. If they manage, they score five points.
- As in the real game of rugby, to score extra points the try needs to be 'converted'. To convert a try, the player places the coin between their index finger and thumb and then spins it, before attempting to catch it mid-spin. Next, someone from the opposition creates 'goalposts' by forming an H with their fingers and thumbs, and the player attempts to throw the coin over the 'crossbar' using their two thumbs. If successful, the player scores another two points.
- First person to score fifty points wins.

# TWO

# Organised Fun for Nature's Playground

Whether you're a Ray Mears type or the sort of person who can't leave their house without their heels, the great outdoors offers a profusion of entertainment delights. From an afternoon on the lawn to a cross-country hike, there's nothing like a few lungfuls of fresh air to boost your spirits and get you raring for a bout of organised fun.

The following chapter bubbles with ideas for games you can play in the garden, field or fen, and will have you abandoning your sofa in no time for the pleasures that can be found in nature's playground.

# Frozen T-Shirt Competition

### What's the game?

Definitely one for the summer. This game involves racing to be the first to put on a frozen T-shirt.

### What do I need to play it?

A T-shirt for every player and a freezer to prepare them in.

### How many friends?

As many as you like.

### How do I play it?

- The T-shirts are thoroughly soaked the day before and either screwed up and tied up into a tight ball or folded up as if to be put away. They are then placed in the freezer overnight. The more water left in the T-shirt, the harder it is to put on, so it's up to you whether you want to wring it out or not.
- Players line up with the frozen T-shirts on the floor in front of them. On the signal, players race to put their T-shirts on.
- The first to get their T-shirt all the way on wins.

# Splat the Rat

### What's the game?

This used to be a staple of any country fair or village fête. Perhaps because my attendance at such quintessentially English occasions has dwindled, I haven't seen it in action for years. It requires a bit of preparation, but the reusability of the equipment makes it worth the time invested.

### What do I need to play it?

A toy rat or mouse, a long tube or piece of drainpipe, a plank of wood, something to fix the two together (such as gaffer tape), a stepladder, and a rolling pin or rounders bat to do the splatting.

### How many friends?

However many you like.

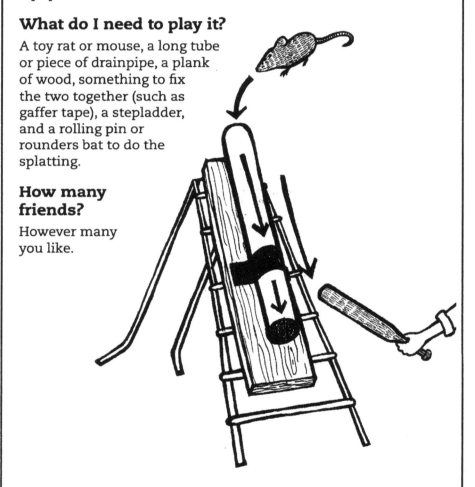

## How do I play it?

- First of all, you need to manufacture your apparatus. Take a long tube about two metres in length – a piece of drainpipe is ideal – and a slightly longer plank of wood, and strap the two together using gaffer tape or similar.
- You need to ensure that the edge of the plank of wood and the drainpipe are aligned and that the plank extends beyond the end of the drainpipe – around fifty centimetres is ideal. This is to provide a 'splatting' area for when the rat shoots out of the the tube.
- You then need to set your game up by resting the plank, with the pipe uppermost, on top of your stepladder.
- Once set up and ready to go, the first player positions themselves kneeling down at the bottom of the pipe with the rolling pin gripped in hand.
- The toy rat is then sent scuttling down the pipe, and the player scores a point if they manage to hit the rat with the rolling pin when it comes out at the other end.

# Human Crufts

## What's the game?

Human Crufts is one of the many brilliant games invented by the wonderful Bestival Festival team at Camp Bestival. The event involves pairs of friends (one of whom pretends to be the pooch and the other the owner) competing in an agility class, a freestyle performance and a beauty contest.

## What do I need to play it?

Some obstacles for the agility course and a range of fancy dress items for the beauty contest. You also need to make some large score cards so that each judge has a sheet of paper with a single number on it from 1 to 10. A dog lead per competing pair is also a useful accessory.

## How many friends?

This one works best in big groups.

## How do I play it?

- Decide on your judging panel (ideally three people) and get everyone else to pair up and decide who's the pooch and who's the owner.
- Pairs then go away and practise their show routine (a freestyle performance of their choosing) and the agility class, and agree on the outfit for their beauty contest.
- Meanwhile the judges set up the obstacle course – think along the lines of planks to balance on, obstacles to jump over and, if you can get your hands on one, a tube to tunnel through.
- Contestants then compete in the three classes and are scored out of ten by the judges, who hold up a score card at the end of each performance.
- The competing pair with the highest score at the end of the competition wins.

# Cow Sniffing

## What's the game?

Much to my mother's fear and loathing, my three siblings and I used to start playing this the minute we arrived at our aunt's house in Devon. Please play with caution and it's totally at your own risk. You have been warned.

## What do I need to play it?

A field full of cows.

## How many friends?

As many or as few as you like.

## How do I play it?

- Find a field of cows. Make sure there are no bulls or bullocks (baby bulls) in there. Young heifers (female cows) are the best as they're intensely curious but without the bullishness of the male variety.

- Lie down next to each other, or on your own if you're playing solo, in a cowpat-free area and close your eyes.

- The natural curiosity of a cow means that within a few minutes (or hours, if it's a hot, lazy day) you will attract the attention of the majority of the herd.

- You must now lay as still and quiet as possible. The player who is brave enough to lie there the longest while twenty dewy, slimy muzzles are pushed in their face wins.

- The perceived saving grace of the game is that the minute someone moves, the herd scatters – hopefully away from you.

# Baby Racing

## What's the game?

The innate competitiveness of most new parents makes this game a winner. If they're not already boasting about six-month-old Junior's maths genius or how little Maisie is already displaying Mozart-like talent on her rattle, then they soon will be. This game puts an end to such speculative boasting and puts the babies and their parents to the test. The baby-owning entry criteria for this game does make it a little exclusive, but you could always borrow one if you were set on playing.

## What do I need to play it?

A few babies, their parents (or carers) and an area in which to race.

## How many friends?

This is a race and entry needs to be in teams of two adults with a baby. To ensure it's a fair match, babies need to be in the same age bracket.

## How do I play it?

- Mark out your racetrack. I'd suggest not being too ambitious with distance at this stage, so set out something around three metres in length.
- Get one adult lined up with the child at the starting point and the other adult positioned at the end of the track.
- On the word 'Go!', babies are released and race (well, that's the idea, anyway) to their adult partner who is waiting at the other end of the track, cooing like a maniac.
- The adult at the end of the track is allowed to make as many encouraging noises as they like to urge the baby on but they are not allowed to use their hands at all.
- The first baby to touch their racing partner's knees at the other end of the track wins.

# Field Raider

## What's the game?

If you are one of those people who needs some gentle cajoling to step away from the computer console to head out on a country walk, then this game is an ideal first foray into homespun fun. It's a bit like Gate Vaulting (see following game), but in this version players are allocated certain obstacles and awarded points each time they're cleared them.

## What do I need to play it?

Some friends (or indeed one friend) who are about to head off on a long country stomp across unknown territory.

## How many friends?

Best played in small groups of two or three.

## How do I play it?

- Before you set off on your walk, agree which obstacle(s) each walker is going to be allocated. You need to be heading off somewhere where no one has been before to prevent an unfair advantage. You should also choose obstacles which will be commonly featured on the type of walk you're doing. For example, if you're going on a cross-country tramp then one player might be allocated a wooden gate, another a metal gate and another a cow's feeding trough. If, however, you're heading off on coastal paths then the obstacles allocated might be a bench, a dustbin or a National Trust sign.

- Players are then awarded points each time they pass and clear their obstacle. You'll also need to agree how each obstacle is going to be cleared. You could leapfrog a bin, balance across a bench and flip over a gate, for example.

- The player who accumulates the most points by the end of the walk is the winner.

# Tug of Love

### What's the game?

My boyfriend and I are constantly competing for our dog's love and affection. Any new set of dog owners would be telling a lie if they claimed they didn't secretly vie to be number one in their little pooch's eyes. This game puts this adoration to the test. I've heard US divorce courts use this method to decide who keeps the dog, but that might be only a rumour. Barney always wins this game, but I know it's total cupboard love and it's me that Otter (that's our dog) really loves the most.

### What do I need to play it?

An umpire, a dog and its two owners.

### How many friends?

See above.

### How do I play it?

- Get the umpire to stand in the middle holding the dog, with the two owners positioned equidistantly on either side. The distance between the two owners should be around ten metres.

- On the word 'Go!', the dog is released and the two owners must make encouraging noises to get the dog to come to them. No treats, toys or food of any kind can be used.

- Whoever the dog goes to first is the winner and clearly the dog's preferred owner.

# Gate Vaulting

## What's the game?

A long country walk can be made far more interesting when turned into an equestrian-style event. Contestants are awarded points for creativity in clearing gates, fences and stiles. Young, lithe urbanites have been jumping on the bandwagon of this game and can be found hurling themselves over buildings (well, small walls at least) and running up lampposts on city streets all over the world. Parkour is a sport that's exploded in popularity among energetic youths and it's even been immortalised in the James Bond film *Casino Royale*.

## What do I need to play it?

An athletic disposition and sporty footwear are both an advantage.

## How many friends?

Can easily be played on your own, though an element of competition with a friend makes it far more entertaining.

## How do I play it?

This one needs very little explanation. While on a country walk, players are awarded points for their creativity in clearing whatever obstacles they come across.

Some advanced jumping styles are shown here. The person with the most points wins.

# Water Bombing

### What's the game?

This is another great game for a blistering day in the afternoon sun. In this version players stand in a circle and when their number is called they must race in and catch the water balloon.

### What do I need to play it?

A whole packet of water balloons filled and tied.

### How many friends?

Great for large groups of five and above.

### How do I play it?

- To get started, someone stands in the middle with everyone else stood in a circle around them. They then number all players including themselves.
- When set up, the person in the middle throws a water balloon up into the air and shouts one of the numbers. That person has to run in and catch the water balloon. If they fail, they're out and have to step out of the circle.
- Before they leave the circle they pick up one of the water balloons and chuck it in the air and shout another player's number.
- The last player left in is the winner.

# Soggy Backs

## What's the game?

If it's a hot sunny day and you fancy a game to cool you down, have a crack at this one. It essentially involves pairs racing to see who can roll a water balloon between their backs down to the floor without bursting it.

## What do I need to play it?

One water balloon per competing couple. If you can't get your hands on water balloons, you could use eggs instead, though they obviously lack the cooling properties of the former and could leave you in a bit of a slimy mess.

## How many friends?

A minimum of four or however many want to play. You just need to ensure everyone is paired up.

## How do I play it?

- Players pair up stand back-to-back with the water balloon positioned between their two shoulder blades. This will obviously vary depending on how big each of the players are, but you just need to make sure the balloons are positioned at the same distance from the ground for everyone.
- On the word 'Go!', players race to manoeuvre the balloon down their backs and safely onto the ground.
- The first pair to complete the task wins.

# Egg Throwing Contest

## What's the game?

Egg throwing is a sport that's enjoyed around the world. The event involves one person throwing an egg for their partner to catch without breaking it over ever-extending distances. The record is currently held by Johnny Dell Foley and his cousin Keith Thomas, both from Texas, who in 1978 threw an egg an impressive 98.51 metres. Each year the annual World Egg Throwing Championship is held in the village of Swaton in Lincolnshire. You too can recreate the dignity and splendour of this event in your own back garden.

## What do I need to play it?

One raw egg per competing pair.

## How many friends?

As many pairs as fancy competing and someone to be umpire.

## How do I play it?

- Pairs of players position themselves an equal distance from each other. I would suggest starting this event off at an easily achievable distance of roughly two metres.

- On the word from the umpire, players take it in turns to throw their egg to their partner. If the egg is dropped, the pair step out of the game.

- Once the remaining pairs have completed the task, all players on one side take a backward step, ensuring they are still positioned at an equal distance from their partners.

- The event plays on until there is one last remaining pair who are then declared the winners.

# Cheese-Rolling

## What's the game?

No one really knows the true origins of the annual Cotswold cheese-rolling event. Some claim it has pagan roots, with others dating it back to Roman times. Held each year in the Gloucester village of Brockworth, the event has grown in size and popularity over the years and contestants travel from all over the world to compete in this slippery and downright painful task, which involves chasing a round Double Gloucester cheese all the way down the hill.

If you're picnicking near a hill or walking along a tussocked slope, you can recreate the majesty of the event yourselves.

## What do I need to play it?

Ideally a large round cheese. As you're unlikely to have one of these stashed under your armpit while stomping through the countryside, you can use whatever you have to hand. We've always used a frisbee, though anything that's round will do. You also need a steep hill to play on.

## How many friends?

As many as are brave enough to compete.

## How do I play it?

- You're a grown-up – well, I'm assuming you are, as this book is written for grown-ups. Anyway, my point is I'm not going to patronise you with words of caution, but obviously don't throw yourself off a cliff or slope. Exercise a degree of common sense.

- Warnings over and done with. Get your contestants lined up at the top of the hill and get your cheese or round object rolling down the hill.

- As soon as it has been set off on its merry way, contestants race down the hill to try to grab it.

- First person to the bottom is the winner.

# Ankle Wars

## What's the game?

This competitive and mildly violent game is ideal to burn off any excess testosterone and put an end to futile debates about who really is the greatest of them all. This is an ankle grabbing and tripping contest in which competitors fight to floor their battle partners.

## What do I need to play it?

Strong ankles and legs.

## How many friends?

As many as want to compete. If there are more than two of you, you can run it as a tournament-style event. I'd recommend one person being the umpire.

## How do I play it?

- First contestants need to remove their shoes and socks and position themselves on some soft ground.
- To prepare for battle, contestants bend down and grasp their ankles with their hands. This position must be maintained throughout the duel. Any contestant who lets go of their ankles is awarded a foul; three fouls and a contestant is eliminated from the competition.
- On the word from the umpire, players must floor their opponent by hooking their legs behind their opponents and tripping them up. Any other manoeuvre is a foul.
- The contestant who floors their opponent is the winner.

# Shoe Tag

## What's the game?

This game used to be one of our favourites while travelling through the delights and wonders of South-east Asia. Its simplicity means that it's easy for anyone to pick up, and it overcomes language barriers as it requires little explanation. It's a great variation on the classic game of Tag and involves you having your shoes – ideally a light summer sandal or flip-flop – stuffed down the back of your trousers, shorts or skirt for the other opponents to grab.

## What do I need to play it?

Players wearing an appropriate item of clothing that their light summer shoes can be stuffed down the back of. If the girls are wearing dresses, you'll need something that can be used to make belts. If you're wearing a bikini, I'd suggest putting a sarong or trousers on as you could end up flashing more than you intended.

## How many friends?

A big rambling gang of you.

## How do I play it?

- Get everyone to put their shoes either down the backs of their trousers or skirts or tucked securely under a belt. You need to ensure that each player has a reasonable amount of shoe sticking out of the top so that the other players can grab it.

- Decide who's 'it'. That person has to chase everyone else and try to pull a shoe out of the backs of their trousers, skirt or belt.

- Once a shoe is grabbed, these are then put at the side and the player who has just lost their shoe becomes 'it'.

- Players are out when both their shoes are taken. The last remaining player is the winner.

# Frolf, or Gisbee

## What's the game?

Some friends devised this game while on a long walk through the Monmouthshire countryside. They thought they'd stumbled on a way to bring golf into the twenty-first century, but soon found it to be a recognised sport in the United States. It's a great way to provide added entertainment to a long walk and requires nothing more than a frisbee and some friends.

If you don't have a frisbee to hand, you can always use a round plastic lid or even a sun-dried cowpat.

## What do I need to play it?

One frisbee per player, some friends and a large area to play in. If you're getting serious about it, then you could craft some large, chain-like hoops to mark the holes around the course, as they do in the States.

## How many friends?

As many or as few as you like.

## How do I play it?

- Each player takes it in turns to pick a marker to be the next Frolf target on the course. Before taking a shot at each target, players must agree on the par (a realistic number of throws that it will take to reach that tree, bush or bin). For example, if you agree a par of three and reach the target in two throws, you are one under par.

- The objective of the game is to travel around the course to each target in the smallest number of throws. The winner is the player with the fewest total throws.

# Water Pistols at Dawn

### What's the game?

This game sees teams compete to successfully direct their blindfolded players to make a direct hit with a water pistol.

### What do I need to play it?

Two water pistols and two blindfolds. It's also handy to have some towels available and some warm clothes if it has the potential to get nippy later.

### How many friends?

Enough to form two teams, though you can play it with as few as four of you. It's also good to have a non-player to act as the umpire.

### How do I play it?

- Get everyone into two teams and position them in two semicircles facing each other with the guns on the ground in the middle. Number each of the contestants in both teams, i.e. both teams should have a number 1, 2, 3 and so forth.

- Once everyone is in position, the umpire announces the start by picking a number and then puts the blindfolds securely on the two contestants assigned this number. On the word 'Go!', they each have to find their way to the pistols directed by their teammates and race to be the first to shoot their opponent.

- The first contestant to make a successful direct hit scores a point for their team. The two contestants go back to their positions in the semicircle and two more players are called forward and the game plays on.

- The first team to reach ten points is the winner.

# Human Croquet

## What's the game?

Another novel alternative to the traditional game of Croquet, without the fuss and bother of acquiring the proper kit. This time the game is played blindfolded, with players adopting the role of the mallet, ball and hoop.

## What do I need to play it?

The only equipment you need for this game is people. To make it work properly you actually need quite a few friends – erm, twenty-two, in fact.

## How many friends?

Ideally you need twenty-two players: ten pairs to be the hoops, one for the ball and another to be the mallet. It is workable with far fewer players, it just means a lot of running around: those who are the hoops have to manoeuvre themselves into a different position once their hoop has been cleared.

## How do I play it?

- Ten pairs of people position themselves around the course facing each other, with their arms raised in the air, clasping each other's hands to create a 'hoop'. If you're playing the game with fewer people, just ask hoop players to move themselves into another position once their hoop has been cleared.

- The 'ball' is then blindfolded and their partner, the 'player', must direct the blindfolded ball through the ten hoops in sequence.

- The player moves the ball by standing behind them, turning them in the intended direction, then saying 'Go!'; no further commands can then be given (or contact made) except for a 'Stop!' command.

- Teams take it in turns to play and the usual Croquet rules apply. In summary, the object of the game is to get the ball through the appropriate sequence of hoops. Players take it in turns to hit the ball around the course. If you get your ball through a hoop in one go (i.e. from 'Go!' to 'Stop!'), you get another turn. If your ball hits an opponent's, they stay where they are while you get another go. If your ball hits the hoop, your go ends and it's the turn of the next player.
- The goal of the game is to get around as many hoops as possible in the right sequential order. The first team to make it around the course wins.

# Fruit Croquet

## What's the game?

A blissful, bizàrre way to spend an afternoon. There's a certain art to directing a croquet ball using only a stuffed stocking swinging majestically between your legs. You'll be pleased to hear that it looks every bit as rude and ridiculous as it sounds.

## What do I need to play it?

A stocking and an apple or orange for each player. You also need something lighter to be the ball. A tennis ball or a light football is ideal. Finally, you need something to create hoops or mini-goalposts with. We've always used pebbles to mark them, but if you've got some time you can create large hoops by bending garden wire into shape and sticking them in the ground.

## How many friends?

A minimum of two and a maximum of eight per game, to prevent it going on too long.

## How do I play it?

- Each player creates their own croquet 'mallet' by putting a piece of fruit in a stocking and then dangling it between their legs by attaching it to their belt. Using your hands is not allowed; players must swing their hips to create a pendulum-like motion with the mallet and thus propel the ball towards the hoops.

- Mark out the route by creating hoops or mini-goalposts around your designated pitch – ideally five or six hoops. You can use pebbles to mark out the hoops, or you can create garden-wire hoops as described above.

- Players then play Croquet following the traditional rules (see Human Croquet on previous page). You only get one go at hitting the ball, unless you go through a hoop and then you get an extra go. If you 'roquet' another player (if you hit their ball with yours), you also get another go. You can only roquet your fellow players' balls once in between each hoop.

# Broom Polo

## What's the game?

As a horse-loving, city-living kid, I spent much of my childhood cycling around car parks on my trusty rusty bike, imagining it was a noble chestnut steed galloping through the countryside.

After coming across the game of Polo in one of my well-worn pony books, my bike–horse game was soon adapted to include our kitchen broom and I persuaded my younger sisters to join me in a game of Broom Polo. We revisited it as adults one gin-soaked summer afternoon and it proved to have held its magic.

## What do I need to play it?

A ball, a bike and a broom per player, with tin cans for goalposts.

## How many friends?

You can play it with two of you, but two teams of four (as in a real game of Polo) is the ideal scenario.

## How do I play it?

- If there are more than two of you, get yourselves into teams. Players mount their bikes and grasp the broom as if it were a polo mallet, with the sweeping end used to hit the ball.

- Each 'chukka' (period of play) lasts seven minutes and you can choose to play between four and seven chukkas, depending on how much time you've got.

- The object of the game is to score goals to win. Hitting the ball with your broom across the line scores a goal. If a ball is knocked by your bike rather than your broom, this also counts as a goal.

- The team with the most goals at end of the chukkas wins.

# Bale Toss

## What's the game?

The Bale Toss is a much-loved village-fête cornerstone that allows a country lad to impress his sweetheart through a showcase of masculinity and strength. It's essentially a competition to see who can throw a bale of straw the highest by lobbing it over a pole that's slowly raised higher and higher.

It was the highlight of my sister Rachel's wedding (obviously apart from the actual marriage and speeches bit) with the entire party gathered to cheer the participants on. Luke, the groom, put in a particularly spectacular performance when his tossed bale failed to make it over the bar and instead landed on his head.

## What do I need to play it?

A long pole (it can be a long stick, piece of fencing, sailboat mast etc), ten metres of strong rope and twenty metres of strong cord, one extending ladder pulled into two separate pieces and a couple of bales of straw. If you want to make your bales lighter, it's good to have some extra string so you can halve the size of the bale and tie it back up.

## How many friends?

You need some strong friends to help you get everything set up and as many competitors as fancy having a go.

## How do I play it?

- First of all you need to get your bale-tossing bar set up. This is essentially a bar that can be easily raised once everyone has cleared it. There are a number of ways you can do it, but my brother-in-law Luke developed the following system:

- Find yourself a good strong fence (a post-and-rail type is ideal) and firmly rope your two ladders onto the fence about three to four metres apart (or the same length as your metal bar) so they point upwards. You need to make sure the rope is knotted tightly as the bale hits the pole with quite a force and you don't want the ladders to fall on people and cause a nasty accident.

- Next, you need to figure out a pulley system. Cut the cord into two equal ten-metre lengths. Attach them to each end of the raising pole. Attach something heavy to the other end of the strong cord and throw this over the top rung of one of the ladders. When you pull on the cord, the raising pole should easily slide up the ladder. You will have to adjust one side at a time, or alternatively have two people at the ready to raise the pole.

- You might find that a whole bale of straw is too heavy to throw for the ladies (and perhaps even the men). If you can track down a horse's hay net, this makes an ideal means to hold a split bale. Alternatively, securely tie up half a bale with rope.

- Once you're all set up, the event plays in rounds. Contestants take it in turns to throw the bale over the pole. If you manage it, you're through to the next round. If not, you're out. The person who can throw the bale the highest is the winner.

# Amy's Competitive Yoga Posing

## What's the game?

Competitive Yoga Posing will have a certain appeal to yoga enthusiasts, but it's equally entertaining to watch yoga virgins attempting to throw and hold a strong move; or indeed for the group to come up with entirely new poses of their own creation. The object of the game is to throw the most impressive but stable yoga position and challenge the other contestants to be the first to pull out. Points can be awarded for dexterity and flexibility as well as endurance, but it's easier to play 'first man down is out'. My friend Amy came up with this one for our first-ever Organised Fun Olympics. It was also a key feature at our most recent Olympics, with my friend Dudgey winning despite being a stonking eight months pregnant. Pretty damn impressive.

## What do I need to play it?

A judge and some competitors.

## How do I play it?

• Players form a circle and take it in turns to throw their chosen yoga move. Everyone must then copy that move. You might

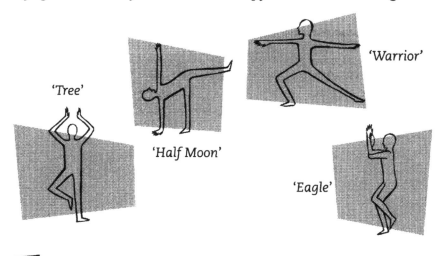

'Tree'

'Half Moon'

'Warrior'

'Eagle'

choose the Tree, the Warrior, or, if you're feeling brave, a Headstand.

- You need to make sure your moves are as challenging as possible, otherwise there will just be a lot of standing around in funny positions.
- The first person to fall out of the position is out, and it's then on to the next person, until the last person standing wins.

# Arcadia's Leap

## What's the game?

We invented this at a friend's birthday on Hampstead Heath. It's great for picnics and other outdoor social occasions.

## What do I need to play it?

A spacehopper is a great addition, but by no means essential.

## How do I play it?

- This is a game of trust as well as jumping ability, as contestants compete to see who can jump over the most friends. Very few rules apply and any jumping style can be adopted.

- Get your first friend to lie on the ground and the contestant leaps over them. After each successful jump, another player lies next to their friend, making the distance to be jumped farther and farther.

- The contestant who jumps the farthest wins.

- When we played it up on the heath, the birthday girl had been given a spacehopper and we used it to give us extra bounce. If you can rustle one up from somewhere, it's a significant addition to the game.

# Schnitzeljagd

## What's the game?

This is a popular German variation of the Scavenger Hunt. Great to instigate when you're setting off on a country stomp but you are at that rather frustrating stage when half the group is still faffing around making sure their hairclips match their wellies. Those who are ready can set off on their merry way leaving a trail for the others to follow.

## What do I need to play it?

Stones, sticks and other bits of nature that can be used to mark a trail.

## How many friends?

At least two of you – the 'hunter' and the 'hunted' – though bigger teams make it more fun.

## How do I play it?

- Before you start, agree on where the game will finish, and ensure the hunted have a collection of sticks, pebbles and chalk to leave their trail.

- Split into two groups, with the hunters being slightly larger in number. The object of the game is for the hunted to reach the designated place before they're caught.

- The hunted are obliged to leave clues along their way to lead and mislead the hunters. The clues must always lead the right way, but you can set false routes as long as they end in a clearly marked X. A selection of other signals are:

- Directional arrow (perhaps made out of twigs).
- A star of arrows to show different possible directions (false and true).
- A chalked X on a tree.
- A ribbon tied to a tree to show you're on the right route.
- If the hunted reach the designated point before being found, they're the winners. If the hunters find them first, they become the winning team.

# Last Bike Standing

## What's the game?

My neighbour Gareth, who lives in the houseboat opposite, told me about this one. He and some friends came up with it on a camping trip. The aim of the game is to try to force your opponents to put their feet on the ground.

## What do I need to play it?

A bike per player.

## How many friends?

You can play it with two, but it's more fun with three or four.

## How do I play it?

- First of all, agree the boundaries of the cycling area.
- The objective of the game is to be the last bike standing. Players are out as soon as they put their feet on the ground.
- To play, players cycle around trying to block each other's paths, forcing their opponents to put their feet on the ground.
- No pushing, hitting or gouging allowed, but other non-violent, non-sportsmanlike tactics are encouraged.

# Tin Can Horseshoes

## What's the game?

This is a traditional English village game honed by the young farmers of Britain. As horseshoes aren't found in abundance in the city, you can also play using empty tin cans or anything that has a ring-like shape.

## What do I need to play it?

For the traditional game, you'll need horseshoes and a metal or wooden stake (or even a sturdy stick) that can be firmly hammered into the ground. If not easily accessible, then clean out some old tin cans and open at both ends. The standard 400g tin cans are in fact pretty tricky to loop over so you might want to use the wider ones or even manufacture yourself a ring using rope or string.

## How many friends?

As many or as few of you as you like.

## How do I play it?

- Get yourself set up by hammering a stake into the ground.
- The object of the game is to get your horseshoe or tin can over the stake.
- Players have three shots to try to hoop it over the stake in the ground to win a prize.

# THREE

# Organised Fun for the Beach, Pool and Campsite

If you're reading this chapter, it probably means you're planning to head off or are indeed already on holiday. Or perhaps you're just a lucky swine with a beach or pool on your doorstep, meaning your life is one long rollercoaster of fun.

Anyway, for a moment I'm going to join you to share the scent of salt water in the air, the sweet aroma of a barbecue, the cawing of the gulls and crashing of the waves, and feel the soft water lapping gently at my feet . . . aaaah!

I'm back. OK. To ensure your holiday or afternoon by the pool is one long jamboree of fun, this chapter is jam-packed with holiday game ideas. Having spent my childhood and much of my adult years honing and perfecting fun in the sun, I have included our tried-and-tested winners for you to peruse and try out at your sunny pleasure. Don't forget to send me a postcard.

# The Sand Dune Grand National

## What's the game?

My boyfriend Barney and his brother Sam developed this sport as children. After spending hours trying to ride sand dunes with their bums stuck in washing-up bowls, their efforts were rewarded with boogie boards as their stepfather looked on encouragingly, hoping they'd soon be following in his surfing footsteps. Instead of immediately taking to the sea, they decided to get these young stallions into training for the Sand Dune Grand National: a race down a sand dune, mounted on a boogie board.

## What do I need to play it?

A boogie board per contestant and a sand dune to race down.

## How many friends?

As many as you have boogie boards for.

## How do I play it?

- Get the racers to mount their boards and position themselves at the top of the sand dune. You can use the arm leash as your reins and you can dig your heels into the sand to provide you with some brakes.

- On the word 'Go!', contestants race to the bottom of the sand dune. The first to the bottom, still mounted on their boogie board, wins.

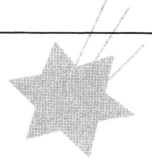

# Dune Jumping

## What's the activity?

Dune jumping is set to go global, following in the fast-paced tracks of its urban older brother Parkour. This activity involves hurling yourself off the top of a sand dune and trying to execute some mid-air manoeuvres. It's worth highlighting that the manoeuvres bit does take some practice. You're more likely to end up with a bruised bum and sand in some uncomfortable places, but also a sense of pride that you braved the challenge and have now joined the ever-growing movement of 'hurlers', as I like to call them, who throw themselves off sand dunes, buildings and urban obstacles in the name of Xtreme Sports.

We first found out about this sport late one night when we were nestled at the bottom of a sand dune, around a campfire, regaling each other with tales of whatever. Out of nowhere the air was filled with Red Indian war cries and our dune was crowned by long shadows as all around the rim stood a threatening gathering of teenage boys. Before we'd managed to grasp what was going on, they were hurling themselves towards us, executing the most impressive mid-air back flips and rolls before landing at the bottom and then blooming well grabbing our bags and running off. In a moment of bravery, I managed to chase after the youngest, grab his ankles and, by shining a torch in his face and pretending we were off-duty police officers, got him to lead us to their tents, which were bursting at the seams with that night's pickings.

Anyway, I'm obviously not suggesting this activity pave your way to a new criminal career, but it's definitely a great way to fill a lazy afternoon on the beach. That is, the jumping bit, not the nicking bags part.

## What do I need?

A sand dune with lots of lovely soft sand at the bottom, a strong constitution and a heroic disposition. Sports shoes of some sort are also a considerable advantage. And I'd suggest tucking your clothes in as much as possible to prevent unwanted sand invasions.

## How many friends?

As many as are brave enough to take part.

## What do I do?

- I feel nervous including this game without giving a word of warning – apologies if this sounds patronising. Use your common sense, don't do anything stupid and be warned: many a hurler before you has broken body parts. Just be sensible.

- Decide who are the jumpers and who are the judges. You might decide all jumpers are judges and are able to cast a vote on each competitor's performance. I'll leave this up to you.

- Next, position yourselves at the top of the sand dune, ideally with an appreciative crowd at the bottom waiting to cheer encouragingly at each performance. Try to get some practice in first on some smaller sand dunes before leaping to this stage.

- On the word 'Go!', each contestant jumps off the sand dune and, if feeling brave enough, attempts to execute a mid-air manoeuvre. A few examples are featured here:

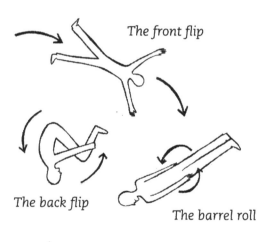

*The front flip*

*The back flip*

*The barrel roll*

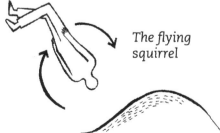

*The flying squirrel*

# Windbreaker Steeplechase

## What's the game?

We invented Windbreaker Steeplechase on a chilly afternoon on.a beach in Devon. In an attempt to brave the British weather, we all purchased a windbreaker and tried to create a den so that we could still enjoy the view without getting blown away. After a certain amount of time, shivering behind a piece of plastic material lost its appeal and we decided to reposition the windbreakers to create a steeplechase circuit for us to race over.

## What do I need to play it?

Some windbreakers, as many as you can get your hands on. If you're on a campsite, check around the bins as people will generally chuck their broken or indeed just used windbreakers away as they pack up and leave. Think of it as recycling.

## How many friends?

As many as are up for taking part.

## How do I play it?

- Position your windbreakers in a circuit. You need to ensure they are a decent distance apart to enable contestants to get the run-up they need.

- Before the race begins, I'd suggest getting your contestants to practise and perfect their styles. A few suggestions are featured below:

  - The flop and roll: throw yourself over the windbreak and break your fall with a forward roll. Good for smaller people.

  - The hurdle: adopt a traditional hurdler style with the front leg straight and leading the way over.

  - The scrabble: just get over any which way you can by throwing yourself at and over the windbreaks, hoping that the faults you incur for knocking them down will be outweighed by the points you score for winning.

- Once contestants have decided on their style, set them up at the starting line and on the word 'Go!' they race around the course. Contestants get a fault point for every fence they hit; three fault points if they knock one down. Faults are deducted from the winning scores. The winner gets three points, second gets two and third gets one. You can of course devise your own scoring system to suit the number and experience of your contestants.

# Sleeping-Bag Sumo

## What's the game?

This is a great camping game. We played it on a Welsh hillside at a farm where a group of us have camped for years. The added element of playing on a slope is that when you're knocked down, you end up rolling down the hill, as it's a nightmare to get up. A word of warning: the smell of cowpats is almost impossible to remove. Choose a sheep-grazed field if you can.

## What do I need to play it?

Sleeping bags and pillows.

## How many friends?

At least two of you, but as many as you want.

## How do I play it?

- Everyone stands in their sleeping bag and grabs their pillow.
- The object of the game is to knock everyone down. Once down, you're out. Last man standing is the winner.
- Get in your sleeping bag with your feet at the closed end. Grab your pillow and start bashing!

# The Organised Fun Olympics

## What's the game?

Each year we hold a much-anticipated Organised Fun Olympics event that takes place over a long, lazy weekend away. Last year we held the event over New Year when we stayed in a house overlooking Crackington Haven beach in Cornwall; this year it's scheduled for a beach camping weekend in Wales. To ensure an even playing field, every contestant comes up with an event, which often means we end up with a three-day decathlon spectacular. From Competitive Yoga Posing to the more sedate evening events such as Competitive Jigsaws (how many pieces can you place in five minutes – don't scoff: it's more fun than it sounds!), the idea is to come up with a programme of activities that everyone can enthuse about and get involved in.

To inspire your contestants to create a truly original event, I've included some of our ideas below, with others featured throughout the book. I'd love to hear what you come up with. To share your plans with others, visit www.organisedfun.co.uk.

## What do I need to play it?

This really depends on the events you choose. My advice is to try to develop ideas that utilise the props and equipment you already have – no need to go out buying expensive bells and whistles. You'll also need some sort of scoreboard; a giant white board is ideal, though obviously rather cumbersome. We usually make ours by sticking a number of A3 sheets together and mounting this on some cardboard.

## How many friends?

As many as want to enter.

## How do I play it?

- For this type of tournament you need to have a very organised person to oversee and facilitate the proceedings. This person should be a respected, trusted and impartial member of your gang and should also act as the final judge on each event.
- Next, decide on your events schedule. We usually do this by email in advance of the weekend, with everyone submitting his or her chosen event. If there are a lot of you, you might need to hold an Event Identification Ceremony, where events are selected from a hat and announced to the gathered contestants.
- A few ideas for events are as follows:
  - Kebab Skewer Darts – see page 58.
  - Windbreaker Steeplechase – see page 54.
  - Competitive Yoga Posing – see page 42.

# Kebab-Skewer Darts

### What's the game?

This game formed part of our annual Organised Fun Olympics one year in Cornwall, and was the deciding game in the tournament.

### What do I need to play it?

A sandy beach and some kebab skewers.

### How many friends?

Works best in small groups of two to eight.

### How do I play it?

First of all, you need to draw out a giant dartboard in the sand. Choose a flat area, with wet, firm sand being best to enable the dart to stand up. To keep it simple I'd suggest drawing three rings, each carrying a certain number of points.

Next, draw a line in the sand at a predetermined distance from the dartboard.

Players then have three goes to score as many points as they can by firing their skewers using the same action as in a game of darts. The obvious warning needs to be added to make sure you play with caution and ensure there are no young children close by.

Depending on how good you get, you need to decide whether a skewer that doesn't stand up in the sand when thrown counts as a point.

# Reverse Stacking-Stones Jenga

## What's the game?

You know how the game of Jenga is all about removing a stick without knocking the tower down? This game turns the rules of Jenga on their head. In this event the challenge is to create the highest stone stack on the beach.

## What do I need to play it?

A collection of stones per contestant.

## How many friends?

As many as want to compete.

## How do I play it?

- The challenge with this game isn't just about being able to stack the highest pile; it's also the competitors' ability to select suitable stacking-stones.

- To get started, each contestant is given fifteen minutes to gather together their stacking stash. Contestants are only able to build from stones they have collected and, if they run out, their stack stops there.

- Once set up, contestants have twenty minutes to create the highest stack, with the tallest being the winner.

# Keep Your Bottle

## What's the game?

A friend's child taught me this game. When inviting me to play, he failed to explain that it would mean I had to sit like an idiot with a bottle on my head while he and his little friends all poured water over me. If it's a simmering summer's day, this game is lots of fun to play for adults as well.

## What do I need to play it?

Two large plastic bottles, two buckets, two towels and two plastic cups.

## How many friends?

Enough to make two teams to make it a race.

## How do I play it?

- Get everyone into two teams and line the teams up. Position one person from each team about four metres away from the lined-up teams, sitting on the ground with an empty bottle held on their head.

- Next, give the person at the front of each line a small plastic cup and a bucket of water.

- On the word 'Go!', the first contestant from each team fills their cup from the bucket and races to the person sitting on the ground. Carefully – or not so carefully – the contestant tries to pour the water from the cup into the plastic bottle on their teammate's head before racing back and handing the cup to the next person for them to carry out the same task.

- The race continues until the buckets are empty. The first team to complete the task is the winner, with extra points awarded to whichever team gets the most water in the bottle.

# Tide Race

## What's the game?

The challenge is to see who can stay on their desert island the longest. Islands are created on a flat sandy beach as the tide is coming in by shovelling and packing sand into piles large enough for you and your teammates to stand on. The winner of the game is the team who manages to stay on their desert island the longest.

## What do I need to play it?

Something to dig with (a piece of driftwood, or your hands would do), and a sandy beach with an incoming tide.

## How many friends?

At least two, or as many as you like. All must be strong swimmers and happy to get wet.

## How do I play it?

- Get into teams of however many you want. Sizes can vary depending on how well you rate your chances of staying on your desert island, based on the volume of people and manpower for building versus the lightness of a single player.

- Each team builds their island, close to the tide on a big flat sandy beach with shallow water.

- Once completed, each team stands on their mound. The team that stays dry on their mound the longest wins.

# Brave the Wave

### What's the game?

My friend Richard, who grew up on the beaches of Norfolk, used to play this as a teenager on the way home from school. It's really a game of daring, hence its popularity among teenage boys. Players compete to be the last one to run from the wave as it crashes on the shoreline.

I recently heard of an urban equivalent called Splash and Dash. Nothing to do with inconsiderate toilet visitors, it instead follows the same rules outlined below but involves large puddles and passing cars.

### What do I need to play it?

A beach with big crashing waves.

### How many friends?

You can play it by yourself if you like, but you might look a bit silly running away from the waves on your own fully clothed.

### How do I play it?

- All line up and face the shoreline on a beach with crashing waves.
- The last person to run away as the waves come crashing in is the winner.
- The alternative is to play it as a knockout. The first person to run away from the waves is out, which does mean a fair share of soaking, but that's all part of the fun.
- An obvious note of safety is required here. Only play on a beach you know well, make sure there's an easy getaway and be absolutely sure there isn't a big rip in the water.

# Beach Sculpture Competition

## What's the game?

Sand-sculpting is an art played out on beaches around the world. Even the sandy banks of the Thames regularly play host to such artists.

A friend came across a Beach Sculpture Competition on a Dorset beach, where the most fantastically imaginative objects were being created. A young Hugh Fearnley-Whittingstall, later to become the celebrity chef, was an enthusiastic participant. Rather than spending hours crafting his sculpture, he went off to do a spot of fishing. Fifteen minutes before the judging took place, he arrived back on the beach with a net full of mackerel. He proceeded to sculpt a voluptuous mermaid's tail over his legs, below his bare torso, and then got his mackerel-filled basket and decorated the tail with a glistening fishy finish. His inspired approach won him the competition and he celebrated by barbecuing his catch and sharing it with his fellow contestants.

## What do I need to play it?

Whatever flotsam and jetsam you can find to fuel your ideas.

## How many friends?

You could easily play it by yourself, but a few friends (as few or as many as you like) make it a lot more fun.

## How do I play it?

- Players are given a set amount of time to create their masterpieces. Part of that needs to be spent scouring for materials.
- At the end of this time, players are judged and prizes awarded.

# Peter Cook's Egyptian Pool Game

## What's the game?

I came across this game in a book about the legendary Peter Cook a collection of stories from some of his friends and colleagues. Stephen Fry, my one and only celebrity idol, had written about a game Peter Cook had invented during a Nile cruise organised by the very generous John Cleese.

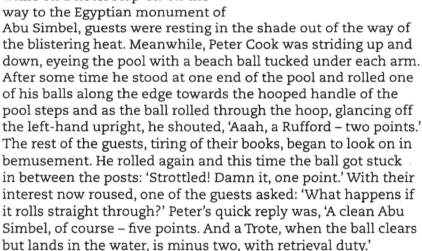

One searingly hot afternoon, while on a hotel stop-off on the way to the Egyptian monument of Abu Simbel, guests were resting in the shade out of the way of the blistering heat. Meanwhile, Peter Cook was striding up and down, eyeing the pool with a beach ball tucked under each arm. After some time he stood at one end of the pool and rolled one of his balls along the edge towards the hooped handle of the pool steps and as the ball rolled through the hoop, glancing off the left-hand upright, he shouted, 'Aaah, a Rufford – two points.' The rest of the guests, tiring of their books, began to look on in bemusement. He rolled again and this time the ball got stuck in between the posts: 'Strottled! Damn it, one point.' With their interest now roused, one of the guests asked: 'What happens if it rolls straight through?' Peter's quick reply was, 'A clean Abu Simbel, of course – five points. And a Trote, when the ball clears but lands in the water, is minus two, with retrieval duty.'

Before long, books were downed and guests and staff had joined Peter to play in what turned into a highly competitive and tense afternoon of Abu Simbel. An international tournament was organised, culminating in the winning team being awarded a vase pilfered by Peter Cook from his hotel room.

## What do I need to play it?

A beach ball and a swimming pool, with either pool steps that feature a hooped handle or a chair that can be positioned by the pool to create the same effect.

## How many friends?

As many as are around to play.

## How do I play it?

- Divide yourselves into teams of around five on each side and identify your goalposts, or position a chair by the side of the pool to create the same effect.

- The aim of the game is to be the first team to reach twenty points. Each player has two bowls or 'Strives' as Peter named them.

- Scoring is as follows:
  - A 'Rufford': when the beach ball clears through the hoop, glances off to one side but doesn't actually go in the water – two points.
  - 'Strottled': when the ball gets stuck in between the posts – one point.
  - A 'Trote': when the ball clears the hoop but lands in the water, – resulting in retrieval duty by the offending player – minus two.
  - 'Abu Simbel': when the ball clears the hoop and passes on through – five points.

- You can of course devise a scoring and naming system to suit your pool environment. As long as the game is played in honour of the legend himself, I'm sure he would approve.

# Water Cricket

### What's the game?

This game is a cross between Baseball and Cricket, played in a swimming pool.

### What do I need to play it?

A swimming pool, a tennis ball and a bat of some sort.

### How many friends?

A minimum of three, though the more the better.

### How do I play it?

- Decide who's going to go into bat first, and who will be bowler. The batter stands at the edge of the pool, while the bowler and fielders position themselves in the water.

- The bowler bowls the ball to the batter from a distance of about four metres. If the batter misses the ball three times, they're out.

- To score two points, the batter has to dive into the water after hitting the ball, swim to where the bowler stands, swim back again and then climb out. To score one point, they must just jump in the water and climb back out again.

- Meanwhile, the fielders have to get the ball back to the bowler before the batter completes this movement. If the ball gets back to the bowler before the batter is back to their base, then the batter is out and it's another player's turn to bat.

- This game continues until everybody has had a chance to bat, and scores are counted up to see who's declared the winner.

# Feet First Race

## What's the game?

This game was invented one summer at my friend Nick's house in France. It was another searingly hot day and Andy came up with a series of games to keep us entertained in the water. It's a novel way to race across the pool and does wonders for your stomach muscles.

## What do I need to play it?

Your good swimming self and a pool to play in.

## How many friends?

As many as you can fit in a race across the pool.

## How do I play it?

- Racers line up, holding the side of the pool, with their feet pushed out in front of them.
- On the word 'Go!', players must swim to the other end of the pool with their feet first and their toes poking out of the water.
- Any deviation from this position is considered a foul: players must pause for three seconds before starting to swim again.

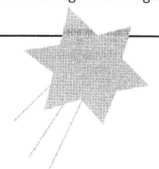

# Pool Pogo

### What's the game?

Another one that arose from that lazy French holiday. This time, players race across the pool by jumping along like a human pogostick.

### What do I need to play it?

A swimming pool and some energetic friends.

### How many friends?

As before, as many as you can fit in a race across the pool.

### How do I play it?

- Get yourselves lined up at one end of the pool.
- On the word 'Go!', players jump towards to the other side of the pool with their hands held behind their backs.
- Racers need to ensure they touch the bottom of the pool on every jump. This is essential to propel yourself across.

# Dugdale's Lilo Surfing

## What's the game?

I've tried this and found it impossible to achieve. As with surfing, you need to invest time and effort to crack it. If you're lucky enough to have a whole summer and regular access to a swimming pool then I reckon you might nail it.

## What do I need to play it?

A swimming pool and two Lilos.

## How many friends?

You can play on your own, or hold a competition when you get good enough.

## How do I play it?

- The basic idea is to surf across the pool balanced on two Lilos. The person who gets the farthest wins.
- To get started, carefully balance two Lilos on top of each other and position them at the side of the pool.
- Next, get out of the pool, stand about three metres back and take a running jump so that your feet land in the middle of the Lilos. Your velocity will propel the Lilos across the pool, and meanwhile you need to balance on top to get as far as you can without falling in.
- Once you've mastered the technique, you can then take it to competition level and see who can get the farthest while remaining balanced on the Lilos.

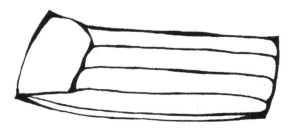

# FOUR

## Organised Fun for Rainy Afternoons

The inclement weather on this fair isle means that a rain-soaked day is more common than one baked by the sun. I've always loved a raging storm; whether it's a reminder of nature's power or because I have a captive audience to join me in some organised fun, I'm not sure. Either way, there are many hidden delights to indulge in during an enforced afternoon tucked up indoors.

If your windows are being rattled and lashed by the elements, don't rage and storm at the ruination of a day. An afternoon by the fire or down at the local pub provides a rich playground of entertainment delights. The following chapter is brimming with ideas and inspiration to make sure you're never at a loss as to what to do when the weather has you holed up indoors.

# Mattress Jousting

## What's the game?

We used to play this at university, when the beds at our halls of residence were adorned with rather flimsy but easily manoeuvrable mattresses. It used to be a favoured feature of our first year until some poor sod managed to tear his, and was forced to sleep on a half-stuffed mattress for the rest of the term. As the corridors were narrow and the walls were bare, the halls provided an ideal environment for endless jousting contests in which we competed to bash each other to the ground.

## What do I need to play it?

For this game, you need an easily manoeuvrable mattress per contestant (inflatable camping mattresses are ideal), i.e. one that you can carry under your arm and run with.

## How many friends?

At least two of you and as many as are up for competing.

## How do I play it?

- Get your first two contestants positioned about ten metres away from each other, with mattresses tucked under their arms and determination in their eyes.
- On the word 'Go!', contestants charge at each other with the intention of knocking their opponent to the ground with their mattress. After each charge, contestants turn around and charge again. This continues until one of the contestants is knocked to the ground and their assailant is declared the winner.
- A word of advice: I used to strap my pillow to my bottom to prevent unsightly bruises.

# Human Fruit Machine

## What's the game?

This one's a novel version of the noisy and now slightly archaic pub favourite. A friend of mine came across it at Bristol's St Paul's Carnival, where a fun-loving father and his three sons had set up a stall. They became the hit of the weekend and earned themselves a packet as people queued up to play. It provides a brilliant afternoon's entertainment and makes a great sideshow at your local fête, festival or party.

## What do I need to play it?

You'll need three bags, each containing the same set of three different fruits, along with an old-fashioned football rattle (obscure, but perfect if you happen to have one). Alternatively, be creative and find or make something that sounds like the spinning of a fruit machine, such as a child's rattle. You'll also need a table and three chairs, and three cardboard boxes big enough for you to lean into (anything about half a metre in height and of similar width is perfect) with their bottoms and lids cut off, leaving the four sides intact – again ideal, but not essential.

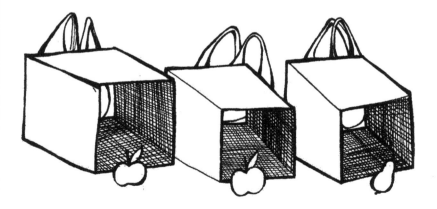

## How many friends?

Four to be the fruit machine and as many as possible to play on it.

## How do I play it?

- Set up the table with three chairs in a row behind it. Place the cardboard boxes on the table next to each other so that when the three players sit down, they can lean into them and be shielded from what the others are doing.

- Get the three players (or the 'fruits') to sit in a line behind the table with their arms leaning into the boxes, and place their bags containing the fruit in front of them. The other player stands to the side of the boxes with rattle (or similar) in hand.

- Punters are then invited to come forward and pay a fixed amount to have a go on the fruit machine. As each punter hands over their money, the 'rattler' makes their fruit-machine noise and the three with the fruit reach into their bags, unseen by each other, and pull out a single fruit item, holding it inside the box so it can be seen by the punter.

- The punter wins an agreed sum if the fruits simultaneously held up are all the same.

# Fruit Boules

### What's the game?

An elegant game of bowls needn't be confined to a summer's day. This refined sport can be rolled out in your living room using your fruit bowl instead.

### What do I need to play it?

You need three of the same type of fruit per player, something to be the jack – a marble or a smaller piece of fruit, such as a plum, is ideal – and some stickers or a pen to identify whose piece of fruit belongs to who.

### How many friends?

However many are stuck indoors with you and can comfortably play a game of boules in your living room.

### How do I play it?

- The game follows the conventional rules of boules but uses pieces of fruit instead of balls. Give each player three pieces of fruit (each player needs to have the same type of fruit to prevent any accusations of unfair play) and get everyone to somehow mark their piece of fruit with a pen or sticker so you know whose is whose.

- Next, decide who's going to bowl first and get this player to bowl the jack (the smaller piece of fruit or marble) to identify the target point everyone is aiming for. The aim of the game is for each player to try to bowl their piece of fruit as close to the jack as possible.

- After the first player has bowled the jack, they then bowl their first piece of fruit and each of the other players take it in turns to follow suit, trying to get as close to the jack as they possibly can.

- After everyone has bowled their three pieces of fruit, the winner is the player whose piece of fruit is closest to the jack, for which they score one point. They also get another point for every piece of their fruit closer to the jack than the nearest piece of fruit of the next successful player.

- The game continues in rounds until someone reaches fifteen points and they are declared the winner.

# Lounge Hockey

## What's the game?

If your imagination has been captured by the idea of adapted indoor sports and you're looking for something a little more active, then give Lounge Hockey a crack. This is a softer adaptation of the classic field sport, using an orange and an umbrella instead of the standard kit.

## What do I need to play it?

An orange and a long umbrella (ideally with a hooked handle) or walking stick per player.

## How many friends?

I'll leave you to decide this, as it really depends on how big your lounge or hall is. In the classic game of hockey there are eleven players in each team.

## How do I play it?

- Get your players into teams and identify who's going to play in field and, if there are enough of you, who's going to be in goal.
- Next, decide where each goal is and where the centre of the pitch is.
- Place the orange in the centre and get two of the players to face each other with sticks poised to hit the ball towards their opposition's goal.
- On the word 'Go!', players tackle and battle each other to get the piece of fruit towards the opposition's goal to score a point.
- It's up to you how long you play for, but to keep it pacey I'd suggest going for ten minutes each way.

# Pants Roulette

## What's the game?

This game came out of our travels around South-east Asia. As the monsoon rains poured down outside, my travelling partner and I lay in our stark room staring up at our ceiling fan. This one only really works if you've got a ceiling fan, so bear it in mind for summer holidays in balmy destinations.

## What do I need to play it?

A ceiling fan and some pants or female scanties.

## How many friends?

As many as are in the room.

## How do I play it?

- Put one pair of pants on a circular ceiling fan while it's turned off.
- Players place bets on which wall the pants are going to fly off and hit.
- Turn the fan on, slowly building up to full speed until the pants are propelled off and splat against the wall.
- Correct guess wins the dosh.

N.B. Different scanties have different velocities when chucked in the air.

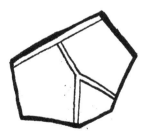

# Supermarket Sweep

## What's the game?

I spent some time living in Sydney, Australia, with a huge rambling group of friends. We made the most of our weekends and holidays by heading off into the hinterland and would regularly hire huge houses in the bush or along the coast to allow us to explore more of that incredible country. On the journey there, we would spend our time planning the huge feasts we would have and write out great long shopping lists to whet our appetites.

As the trips to the supermarket were always a mission – a chore we wanted to get through as quickly as possible to allow us to finally reach our weekend retreat – we devised a game that would have us racing around in the quickest time possible, awarding the winner a free pass from weekend washing-up.

## What do I need to play it?

You need to be going to a supermarket to embark on a huge shop.

## How many friends?

This depends on the size of your list. We would generally divide ours into four with four people playing.

## How do I play it?

- Divide a sheet of paper into four and get everyone to shout out the items they want from the supermarket, and take it in turns to place each item on one of the four lists.

- When you arrive at the supermarket, separate the four lists, fold them up and get each player to choose one.

- On the word 'Go!', players must peg it round the supermarket, trolley in hand, aiming to be the first to make it to the checkout with all the items on their list. Whoever gets there first gets out of paying or washing-up for the weekend.

# Pillow Fight

## What's the game?

Pillow fights are synonymous with rosy-cheeked Enid Blyton characters bashing each other in their tents as Timmy the dog barks around their ankles. In recent years, pillow fights have undergone a resurgence thanks to the effervescent bunch of flash mobbers who surprise the general public by simultaneously turning up at famous landmarks to sing, dance and hold mass pillow fights.

You too can recreate the anarchy of a pillow fight in your living room. To give the event some form and structure, suggested rules are set out below.

## What do I need to play it?

A pillow per contestant and a stopwatch.

## How many friends?

At least two of you to fight and one person to be the umpire.

## How do I play it?

- Fighters stand facing each other with their pillows at the ready.
- On the word 'Go!', they start bashing each other over the head and body with the sole objective of disarming their opponent.
- If no one has been disarmed after one minute, battle is stopped and restarted, but this time pillows must be held with one hand only.
- The first person to disarm their opponent is declared the winner. A tournament-style event can be run if there are more than two competitors.

# Walling

### What's the game?

This is a great challenge to decide who's got the greatest ...
errr... arm strength.

### What do I need to play it?

A wall to lean towards.

### How many friends?

As many as want to partake.

### How do I play it?

- The challenge in this game is to be the person who can stand
  furthest away from the wall while leaning against it and then
  push back into an upright position.

- To get started, players stand at an equal distance away from
  the wall with their feet in a fixed position. On the word 'Go!',
  they lean into the wall with their arms outstretched. They
  must then push themselves back into an upright position.

- Once everyone is upright again, contestants take it in turns to
  take a step back and repeat the move again until they collapse.

- The player who successfully completes the manoeuvre with
  their feet furthest from the wall is the winner.

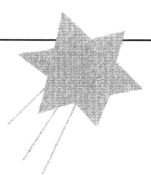

# Catchphrase

### What's the game?

Remember the ITV gameshow *Catchphrase*? Well, now's your chance to relive those moments of TV gold by recreating it on your sofa.

### What do I need to play it?

A couple of pads of paper, some pens and a stopwatch.

### How many friends?

As many as want to take part.

### How do I play it?

- To play Catchphrase at home, a little preparation is required. First of all you need to write out a list of well-known phrases on slips of paper, fold these up and put them in a hat or bowl. You might choose something like 'Rising damp' or 'A weight off my mind'. Write down as many of these as you can. The number you have decides the length of the game.

- Next, get your players to split into two teams and decide who's going first. Each team has sixty seconds for one of their players to choose a slip of paper out of the hat and then try to communicate the phrase to their teammates using illustrations. As soon as their team have got the right answer, they grab another slip of paper and repeat the process. Teams score one point for every correct guess. Once the minute is up, it's then the other team's turn to play.

- Once the other team's minute is up, play reverts to the first team, where another player takes a turn at drawing clues to the phrases selected.

- The team with the highest number of points once all the slips of paper have been used is declared the winner.

# Biggest Forehead

## What's the game?

The aim of this contest is not a 'who's got the biggest spam' competition (now, that *was* a favourite at my school); instead it's a betting game in which players guess the value of a card stuck on their forehead.

## What do I need to play it?

A pack of cards, some betting money (real or Monopoly) and ideally, if you can dig some out, some double-sided sticky tape.

## How many friends?

Great for groups of four to eight.

## How do I play it?

- Get everyone sat around the table and deal each person one card laid face down. Give them each some double-sided tape and get them to stick their card to their forehead without looking at it. If tape is hard to come by and your card is light enough, then the old lick-it-and-stick-it trick might work.

- The aim of the game is for players to bet whether the card stuck on their forehead is the highest one. Unless a player is adept at reading the pack, this is really down to luck, bluffing or telepathic powers.

- Once everyone is set up with cards on heads, each player takes it in turns to place their bets on whether they think their card is the highest (ace is high in this game). If as you look around everyone else's cards you think you've got a high card or are feeling particularly brave, then lay down a high bet. If you think you're at the lower end of the scale then lay a low bet.

- Once bets are placed, players remove the cards from their heads and the player with the highest card scoops up the winnings.

- The game plays on until players have lost all their money or walk out in frustration.

# The Price is Right

## What's the game?

Whether you're lounging at home or sheltering in a pub from the misery that is the British weather, a newspaper is never far away. Recreate the magic of this 1980s ITV classic by guessing the price of items in adverts. This should take about ten minutes – its entertainment value does wear thin if the game goes on for too long.

## What do I need to play it?

A healthy pile of newspapers and magazines and a credit card.

## How many friends?

Works best with three or four of you.

## How do I play it?

- Decide who's going to be the game host and cut out a selection of adverts from magazines or catalogues, making sure the items have their prices displayed, and have a credit card at the ready.
- Position each ad in front of the group and use the credit card to cover up the amount. Players take turns to guess the price they think the item is advertised at, and then the host reveals the real price. Two points are awarded for a correct answer or one point for the person who is closest to the advertised amount.
- First person to score ten points wins.

# Blow Football

### What's the game?

This takes a little bit of time to set up, but if you're a footie fan, it's worth the effort. An ideal substitute to table football.

### What do I need to play it?

Ideally, a decent-sized table to play on, but if this proves difficult you can build your pitch on the carpet. For table play you need lots of strips of cardboard about ten centimetres in height, enough to go all the way around the table, and some tape that won't damage the woodwork to fix them in place. If you're playing on the carpet, the simplest set up is to use T-shirts rolled up in long lengths to create the pitch barriers. You also need a ping-pong ball and straws for each player.

### How many friends?

Ideally played with two opposing players or two teams of two.

### How do I play it?

- First of all, get yourself set up by either taping the cardboard strips to the sides of the table or laying out lines of T-shirts to create the barrier for the pitch. You need to leave goal-sized holes at each end for the ping-pong ball to satisfyingly fly through when triumphantly scoring a goal. Decide how long the match is to last.

- Next, place the ball in the middle of the table, with the two teams stood at either end.

- The aim of the game is to score a goal by blowing the ping-pong ball through the opponent's goal by blowing through your straw, without moving from behind the end of the table. It's also against the rules to use your hands or touch the ball with your straw or face. All scoring and defending must be achieved with the player's own blowing power.

- If you're playing on a particularly long table, you might want to agree that players are allowed to move a little further up the sides of the table. Use a chair or something similar to mark the maximum distance they can move along.

- One point is awarded for each goal scored. Once scored, the ball is placed back in the centre of the table, and play recommences on the word 'Go!'.

- If the ball is blown off pitch, it should be placed back on at the point at which it went out of bounds – pretty much like in a real game of football.

- Play continues for the length of the pre-agreed time period and the player (or players if you're playing in pairs) with the most goals at the end is declared the winner.

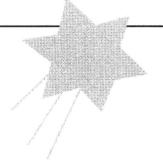

# Are You There, Moriarty?

### What's the game?

This is a Victorian parlour game in which two players take part in a duel. You need to make sure you have enough space to play it. A few friends and I caused some rather nasty damage when we last played, so do be careful.

### What do I need to play it?

Two blindfolds and two rolled-up newspapers.

### How many friends?

Two to play, and as many as are around to watch and wait their own turn.

### How do I play it?

- Get everyone to sit around. Blindfold the duelling pair and get them to lie parallel on their backs, with about a metre of space between them. A good way to measure if there's enough of a gap is to get them to shake hands as a mark of respect for their opponent before duelling begins.

- The starting player then shouts, 'Are you there, Moriarty?' and the opponent responds, 'Yes'. At this signal, the players then attempt to bash their opponent with their rolled-up newspaper while maintaining the same flat position on the ground, without moving their legs or backs.

- The first player to be hit is out and the next player steps in to take their place.

# Dress-Up Sunday

## What's the game?

This is less of a game and more of a way to entertain yourself and a group of friends. It's completely purposeless other than to show off your creative skills in putting a fancy-dress outfit together.

## What do I need to play it?

Some creative flair or some cash to spend at the fancy-dress shop.

## How many friends?

You'd look a bit silly on your own, so I'd suggest at least two of you, though a big group makes it much more fun.

## How do I play it?

- Choose the theme.
- Ask your friends to meet you at the restaurant of your choice all trussed up in your fancy-dress creations.
- If you don't like them, don't turn up. That was a joke. That would be very cruel.

# FIVE

# Civilised Organised Fun for Dinner Parties

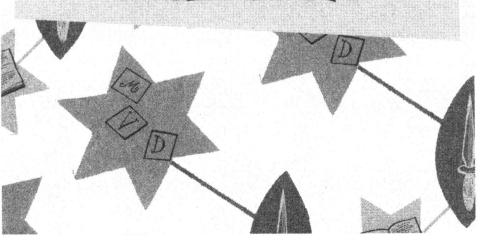

The twilight hours, after the dinner-party feasting is over, is often when people like to indulge in a spell of organised fun. Merry guests, satisfied with their feast, have perhaps exhausted the obvious avenues of conversation and are at risk of being dragged into a deep state of slumber by their full bellies.

The type of games you choose to indulge in will of course depend on your gathered company, and indeed their state of inebriation. If you were holding a civilised affair, perhaps attended by your new boss or other dignitaries, a more cerebral choice would be appropriate – one that highlights your intellect and wit, while also giving your guests a chance to shine. If, however, it's a gathering of old chums, you might wish to reach for a game that enables you to indulge your more theatrical side and laugh at your friends making fools of themselves. Laugh with them, not at them, I mean, of course.

The following chapter is politely simmering with an eclectic collection of the more refined entertainment delights, the type you can happily roll out in civilised company and which will leave your guests gently clamouring for more.

# Culture Vulture Ping-Pong

## What's the game?

If you're looking for an erudite line in after-dinner entertainment, something that perhaps enables you to demonstrate your scholarly ways, then Culture Vulture Ping-Pong could be just the ticket. The game is a ping-pong battle of the brains to come up with titles of books, plays or films that are linked together through words.

## What do I need to play it?

Your finest cultural brain and some pens and paper to keep tabs on the score.

## How many friends?

Ideal for an intimate dinner-party gathering.

## How do I play it?

- The aim of the game is to score as many points as possible by linking the titles of books, plays or films that feature the same words.

- The first person to go nominates the title of a book, play or film. The rest of the players must now rack their brains to find a title of another work featuring one of the words just mentioned. If for example the first player was to say 'Black Beauty' someone else might volunteer 'American Beauty' or 'The Woman in Black'. Each correctly nominated title scores a point.

- The game plays on, bouncing around the table as guests compete to come up with the most connecting titles. The first person to get to twenty points wins.

# Oooh, Betty, the Cat's Done a Whoopsie

## What's the game?

If you're with a group who are hot on their celebrities or literary greats, this game is a winner. Players take it in turns to assume the personality of a famous person and the rest of the group ask questions as if they're meeting them for the first time.

## What do I need to play it?

A working knowledge of famous people.

## How many friends?

Great for a small gathering of four to eight.

## How do I play it?

- Ask each of your guests to think of a famous person they know well, that they feel they could effectively embody. This might be through their language or mannerisms, or perhaps through parodying the way they look.

- The first person to go announces that they are in character and then the rest of the gathered guests must ask him or her a series of questions, as if they were meeting the person for the first time. The guest must then respond to the questions in character, with the others attempting to guess who it is.

- The player who successfully guesses the famous person is the next person to go.

- If you're keen to add a competitive element, you can use a points system in which players score four points if their person is guessed in thirty seconds, three points if within a minute, two points if within ninety seconds, and one point if within two minutes.

# Dudgey's Dirty Dinners

## What's the game?

I think this game could be the driving force behind my friend Dudgey's splendiferous cooking talents. Her thrifty Edinburgh student days meant supper was scraped together from the dregs and fluff left in the larder. Tinned tuna kedgeree and sausage and Branston Pickle pasta were staple features of the student-house menu.

For those familiar with *Ready Steady Cook*, this follows a similar format. Two chefs, three ingredients each and some creative cookery to rustle up a supper that will delight and win the guests' votes.

## What do I need to play it?

Each guest must bring an ingredient with them. A selection of basic culinary essentials should also be available – salt, pepper, oil, garlic and so on.

## How many friends?

Ideally eight: two chefs, and six people who each bring an ingredient and also have the pleasure/displeasure of judging the food.

## How do I play it?

- Guests arrive bearing one cooking ingredient each. Two should be told to bring a protein-based item, two a carbohydrate-based item, and the other two a random, 'curveball' ingredient of their choice.
- The chefs are then challenged to cook a dish each in an agreed time period using the collected supplies. Distribute the food among each of the competing chefs, ensuring that each chef has something from each food group described above. Chefs are then told which course they're cooking.
- The chefs are judged and awarded points for taste, creativity and skill.

# Call My Bluff

## What's the game?

If some of the earlier games are too banal for you, Call My Bluff is a more relaxed and generally more civilised option, which requires players to draft a plausible fake dictionary definition for a wacky or unusual word.

## What do I need to play it?

A dictionary.

## How many friends?

At least three of you.

## How do I play it?

- Players take it in turns to lead each round. Each leader chooses an obscure word from the dictionary, one which they're fairly certain no one knows the definition of.

- All the guests need to write a plausible definition for the word. The objective of the game is to confuse other players into selecting yours as the correct one. If you have an inkling of what the actual definition is, then write this out as if correct. It'll earn you extra points.

- When the definitions are complete, everyone secretly submits them to the holder of the dictionary. The dictionary holder needs to write out the actual definition on another slip of paper to prevent players easily guessing the correct one.

- Each definition is then read out and players must guess which is the right one. Scoring is as follows:
  - All players choosing the actual definition get two points.
  - Players also get a point for each person who selects the definition they wrote.
  - If no one identifies the correct definition, the leader of that round gets a point.
  - If someone has written a definition that is close to the real one, that person also gets two points.
- The game then moves on with different people leading each round. Once everyone has had a go, the player with the highest score wins.
- It's hugely important that everyone writes as clearly as possible, as if a player can't read someone else's writing when it's their turn to read the definition out, they're likely to give away the fact that it's not the actual one.

# Name That Song

## What's the game?

This is a test of musical knowledge. The object is to think of a song with a certain word in the title or lyrics.

## What do I need to play it?

Just yourselves.

## How many friends?

Ideal for two or more players.

## How do I play it?

- Decide who's going first and get them to choose a word (ideally not too hard at the beginning). The other players have to think of a song that features that word.

- Whoever comes up with a song first gets a point, and it's then their turn to choose a word.

- If the group can't think of a song featuring the word that's been put forward, they shout out 'Challenge!', and the person who came up with the word has to sing the song line they were thinking of that features the word. If they manage to do so, they get a point and another go. If the challenged player can't sing a song line featuring their nominated word, they then lose a point.

# Wink Murder

## What's the game?

A game of little effort involving death by winking.

## What do I need to play it?

A paper and a pen.

## How many friends?

More than three but hard to play with over twenty.

## How do I play it?

- First off, write out a slip of paper for every player, ensuring you have one M for 'murderer' and a D for 'detective', with the rest of the pieces featuring a V for 'victim'.
- Put all the pieces in a hat and get everyone to pick one out.
- If you're the detective, your objective is to spot the killer; if you're the murderer, it's to kill everyone with the evil wink of your eye; and if you're the victim, you die a blood-curdling death as soon as someone winks at you.
- The game ends when the detective spots who the murderer is.
- Repeat the game with the roles swapped around. The winner is the detective who manages to spot the murderer with the smallest number of victims.

# You Have a Face

## What's the game?

If you're proud of your loquacious vocabulary and take pleasure in showing it off, this game is for you. This game is a test of your knowledge of adjectives. If you run out of words, you're out.

## What do I need to play it?

A sound knowledge of the alphabet and a decent (or not so decent) grasp of vocabulary.

## How many friends?

As many as are seated around the table.

## How do I play it?

- To get started, the group collectively nominates a letter.
- The first person to go remarks to their neighbour, 'You have a face!' The neighbour enquires, 'What kind of a face?' And the first player replies using an adjective beginning with the appointed letter. So if the nominated letter is 'A' then 'An amphibian face' would be a suitable response.
- The owner of the amphibian face then says to their neighbour, 'You have a face!' and the game goes around, knocking out players who can't think of an adjective beginning with that letter.

# The Shaving Game

## What's the game?

This is a game of trust in which players demonstrate their shaving prowess. Men will obviously be at an advantage, though it's a different ball game when you're shaving someone else.

## What do I need to play it?

Shaving or squirty cream, and a cloth for each of the shavers to wipe their cream onto. A blunt knife (or plastic spoon) and blindfold for each pair.

## How many friends?

As many pairs as you like.

## How do I play it?

- Start off pairing people up as teams (male and female, husbands and wives, girlfriends and boyfriends will work).
- One of the pair sits down while the other is blindfolded, and the blindfolded player applies shaving cream to the seated player's face.
- Once prepared, the blindfolded player continues by attempting to shave their partner using a plastic knife or similar implement.
- The person who did the best job within the set time period wins.

# Two Degrees of Separation

## What's the game?

You need to be with the right type of group to play this game as it has the potential to unearth some unknown truths about some of your friends. The game follows the same theory as for the now-famous Kevin Bacon Game (see page 188) but instead uses your friends.

## What do I need to play it?

Some pens and paper and a gathering of sociable friends.

## How many friends?

Works best in a medium-sized group of between two and ten.

## How do I play it?

- Get everyone to write out the names of ten people they know and put these in a hat. Encourage everyone to think beyond their immediate group but to stick with people they know the gathered party will know. You'll find some of them will be repeated but this isn't a problem.

- Next, guests take it in turns to pick out two names. They then need to identify two steps to connecting these friends before pulling out another two slips of paper. They must do as many pairings as they can in a minute, with one point being scored for each pairing. If you can't come up with a connection then the names go back in the hat and your go ends, and you score points based on the number of connections you've made.

- You need to decide at the beginning what your connections are. Here are some suggestions:
    a. Have kissed
    b. Have more than kissed
    c. Have been roommates

# Theatrical Chinese Whispers

## What's the game?

This game was invented by my siblings and cousins after boring our parents rigid with incessant demands to play Chinese Whispers at our dinner table. By bending the rules slightly we liberated ourselves from our seats.

## What do I need to play it?

Just yourselves, but if you want to go to town you can bring in all sorts of props.

## How many friends?

Definitely more than three of you.

## How do I play it?

- Everyone splits into two teams. Team A goes out of the room and Team B thinks of an action or sequence of actions, which can be as mundane or as dramatic as you like, for example pruning the roses or winning the Grand National.

- One member of Team A returns to the room. The sequence is acted out in front of them by a member of Team B.

- Another member of Team A returns to the room. The first member of Team A then needs to act out their interpretation of what they've seen to their team member.

- And so the sequence goes on, until the last team member enters the room, sees the sequence acted out and has to guess what the performance is about.

- The game then plays on, with the other team going outside.

# Dough You Know What It Is?

## What's the game?

If you're bored of the classic game of Charades and fancy something a little different, this one's a great alternative and, to my mind, a whole lot more amusing. Some friends and their kids came and stayed with us one weekend and the kids brought along their play dough, a soft, clay-like substance that doesn't go hard when you make shapes out of it. We were taking it in turns to demonstrate our sculpting ability when it occurred to us that there was a brilliant game in this.

## What do I need to play it?

Ideally, you need a different colour play dough for each team. If you're struggling to get your hands on any, you can make some salt dough, which works in the same way. Simply mix together three cups of flour, one cup of salt, four cups of water and one tablespoon of glycerine (available from chemists or supermarkets). You can then add food colouring so that each team has a different colour.

The easy alternative is to use Blu-Tack. You'll also need some pens and paper and a hat or bowl to put the slips of paper into.

## How many friends?

Works for small- to medium-sized groups of between four and twelve.

## How do I play it?

- The object of the game is to be the first team to guess a word sculpted out of dough by their teammate.

- To start off, you need to get one person to write out ten things for each of the players in the game. Make sure that all suggestions can feasibly be sculpted out of dough. Put these in a hat or bowl in the middle of the table.

- Next, get yourselves into teams. The ideal number in each team is three, but as long as there are more than one you can make it work.
- Each teammate takes it in turns to be the dough sculptor for the team. Decide who's going first, and that person pulls a slip of paper out of the hat, looks at it and then passes it on to the player in each team whose turn it is to sculpt.
- On the word 'Go!', the sculptors simultaneously start squeezing, crafting and shaping their dough to somehow communicate what the word is. It's up to you whether you allow animation of the dough – animating a bird so it flies through the sky by waving it around in the air, for example.
- The very clear rule, however, is that communication must be through the dough model and any other sort of body action is not allowed.
- The first team to guess correctly wins a point. The first team to ten points wins.

# Ellie's Brilliant Name Game

## What's the game?

This is a guaranteed hit for any occasion and will have people engrossed for a good couple of hours. It's my wonderful friend Ellie's favourite game and is traditionally rolled out at her family Christmas each year. Another winning alternative to Charades.

## What do I need to play it?

A hat, pens and paper.

## How many friends?

Two or more – no limits – but it might get a bit boring waiting for your turn if there are quite a few of you.

## How do I play it?

- Get everyone to split into two teams.
- Each player tears a piece of paper into between five and ten small pieces (depending on how long you want the game to go on for) and writes the name of a famous person on each piece – fictional or real. All pieces of paper are then put into a hat or bowl in the middle of the table.
- The team going first chooses a player to start, who takes a piece of paper from the hat and describes the person on the paper to the rest of their team without mentioning their name. They can do anything but say the name on the paper. Impressions and 'sounds like' clues are allowed.

- They continue doing this for one minute, describing as many names as they can get through. If their team guesses correctly, that name goes into a small pile. If they can't get it, it goes back in the hat. At the end of the sixty seconds, the number of correct guesses is counted up and this is the score for that team. Pieces of paper that have been correctly guessed are put aside.
- It's then someone on the next team's turn and the game plays on, swapping between teams until all the names have been used up.
- The game then goes into round two, The same process is gone through again, using the same names as before, but this time team members are only allowed to say one word to enable others to try and guess what it is. For example, if the character was Marilyn Monroe and it was mentioned in the previous round that 'she was the film star in that famous shot where she's stood on the grille with her skirt blowing up', then you might choose to just say 'skirt'.
- In the final round players have to mime each character, hoping that their teammates remember them from the two previous rounds.
- The team with the highest score wins.

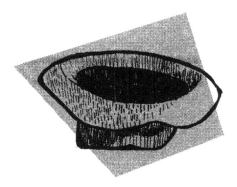

# Kate's Drawing Game

## What's the game?

You might be fooled into thinking artistic types will have an advantage in this game, but their attention to aesthetics is in fact a hindrance. If you can hold a pencil, you can play this. Barney's aunt Kate devised the format for this game one Christmas. Teams have to guess the word their team member is drawing. Brilliant for big, boisterous groups, but easily scaled down too.

## What do I need to play it?

Some pens and paper.

## How many friends?

Great for groups large and small. You'll need one person to act as facilitator.

## How do I play it?

- First of all, you need a list of subjects to draw. I'd suggest coming up with words around four themes, for example food, films, history, literature, and so on. You can get as obscure or as personal as you like. A section on Granddad's bad habits might be interesting, for example. As you write your list, you need to be sure that your words aren't too 'out there' or, more importantly, too hard to draw.

- Split everyone into two teams (or even more if you're playing in a large group), and position the facilitator somewhere in a room that's equidistant between them.

- On the word 'Go!', players on each team take it in turns to race out to the facilitator, each be given the same word and race back to draw it out for their team members, who have to guess what it is. Players mustn't speak (obviously), mime or write down the word. Only drawing is allowed. It's up to you whether players can draw an ear and give 'sounds like' clues.
- As soon as they guess correctly, another player races out to get the next word from the facilitator before racing back and drawing it out.
- The first team to correctly guess all of the words wins.
- If you're a little concerned about how trustworthy each player is, I'd suggest having an umpire who sits in each room to ensure no cheating.

# The Book Game

## What's the game?

This game should appeal to the literati. It's perfect to play if you've hired a holiday cottage, as there is often an eclectic and sometimes comedic collection of books that past guests have left behind.

## What do I need to play it?

A selection of books – include some obscure ones for added interest – and a pad and pen per player.

## How many friends?

At least three of you.

## How do I play it?

- Put the selection of books in the centre of the table and ensure each player has a pad and pen.
- Players take it in turns to lead a round, each selecting a book and reading out the title, blurb and author's name.
- The rest of the players must then imagine what the book's first line might be and write it down. The object of the game is to dupe the rest of the players into thinking your first line is the real one.
- Whoever is leading the round must also write down the actual first line before collecting everyone else's and adding theirs to the pile. They must then take each one and read them out in turn, as convincingly as possible.

- Players must guess which one they think is the real first line. Points are awarded as follows:
  - Two points if someone guesses the right line.
  - One point to a player if someone chooses their fake opening line.
  - If nobody picks the true first line then the person who is leading that round scores two points.
  - Finally, players get five points if they write down the correct first line for the book. It sounds unlikely but it has happened!
- The game moves around with each person taking it in turn to lead.
- N.B. As with Call My Bluff, everyone needs to write as clearly as possible, as if a player can't decipher the writing when they read the lines out it will be obvious that it's a fake.

# Slap My Yodel

## What's the game?

This game came from a skiing trip in the Austrian mountains and is an adaptation of one I picked up on my travels. The first time we played it was with a mixed group of English, German and Swiss friends. Towards the end of the game the English were the only ones left playing and rolling around at the hilarity of it all, while our European compadres stared on in bemusement.

## What do I need to play it?

A forfeit for losing players, such as a drinking forfeit. You also need to be sitting at a table.

## How many friends?

Great for groups of between six and twelve. Any more and it can get a bit boring waiting for your turn.

## How do I play it?

- Get everyone to sit in a circle around a table with their hands placed in front of them. Next, get everyone to lift their left hand and cross it over the arm of the person to their left.

- The first person to go slaps the table and the person to their left slaps the table using the hand that is lying next to the one that did the last table slap. The slapping must then progress around the table in an unbroken circle. This sounds easy, but with your arms crossed it gets very confusing, particularly when the pressure is on.

- A player can confuse things by choosing to slap the table twice at any moment. This sends the slapping in the opposite direction. If someone chooses to slap the table three times during the game, the player next to them according to the order of play has to stand up and yodel, before sitting back down and sending the table slap around in the same direction as before.

- If someone gets it wrong, they get a forfeit.

- The idea is that the table-slapping speeds up as the play goes on, causing complication and confusion as people keep track of what's going on.

- You can add further actions depending on how complicated you want to make it. Alternatively, if you're playing in a really big group, you can start another slap on the opposite side, meaning that players have two games they have to watch.

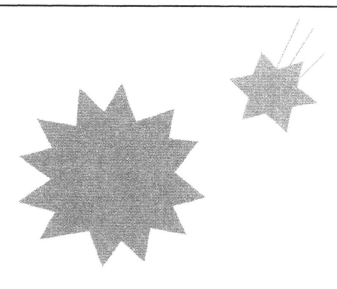

# The Rizla Game

## What's the game?

Amazingly, since I first encountered this as a teenager, this actually turns out to be another of those delightful Victorian parlour games. It's synonymous with my time at university as it was the perfect distraction from our studies and helped fill lecture-free hours and late-night sessions.

## What do I need to play it?

A packet of Rizlas (the larger ones are the best) and some pens to write on them.

## How many friends?

Best played with more than three.

## How do I play it?

- Everyone chooses a character – fictional or real, living or dead – and writes the character's name on a Rizla, before sticking it to the forehead of the person sat next to them without them seeing the name. I'd suggest asking the person to lick and stick it themselves, as the thought of someone else's saliva festering on your forehead is a mild distraction from the game.

- Players must then take it in turns to ask the group a 'yes' or 'no' question to help them guess who they are. The other players are not allowed to say anything other than 'Yes' or 'No'.

- If they get the question right, they're allowed to ask another one. If they get it wrong, it moves on to the next person's go. As soon as a person correctly guesses who they are, they're out.

- The loser is obviously the last one out.

# Louis' Beer Pong

## What's the game?

This is hugely popular with American students and is played out in campuses across the States. It's also a favourite among bar staff in the UK as a means of divvying up tips at the end of the night.

## What do I need to play it?

An oblong table, thirty-two empty plastic or paper cups, two ping-pong balls and some beer if you want to introduce a drinking element to the game.

## How many friends?

Best played with two pairs, or one on one.

## How do I play it?

- Each player or pair lines up sixteen cups to create a ten-cup triangle with six cups balanced on top.
- If you want to introduce the drinking element, put some beer in each of the cups.
- Players then take it in turns to stand at opposing ends of the table and shoot the ping-pong ball so that it lands in one of the cups. Players can either use a straight lob, or as you get better at it you might decide to introduce a bounce, which makes it slightly harder.
- If successful, the opposing team has to drink from the cup containing the ball, and this cup is then removed from play. If the drinking element is not included, the cup is simply moved out of the way.
- The winning team is the team to remove all their opponents' cups from the table.

# Taboo

### What's the game?

Taboo is a civilised word game that's ideal to play around the dinner-party table. It's an old favourite that we regularly roll out as it's easy to explain and people soon catch on.

### What do I need to play it?

Pens and paper and a stopwatch.

### How many friends?

Ideal for small to medium-sized groups.

### How do I play it?

- Get yourself prepared by writing out a list of words (I'd go for about ten per player) and two related words, for example for an oak tree they might be 'green' and 'trunk'. Cut them up into slips of paper (with the main word and the two related words on the same sheet) and pop them in a hat.

- Get the players to split into teams. This works best with a maximum of five in a team.

- The first team to go starts by pulling a slip of paper out of the hat. He or she then has one minute to describe the word on the slip of paper without actually mentioning any part of the word they're describing or the two related words. As soon as the other team members have guessed the word, the player pulls out another slip of paper and tries to get through as many words as he or she can in one minute.

- Once the minute is up, players count up the number of words they managed to describe and play moves on to the next team.

- The game continues until everyone on each of the teams has played. The team with the highest score wins.

# Mind Readers

## What's the game?

This game is a test of your mind-reading prowess – or a demonstration of your deep telepathic connection with your partner. The aim of the game is to guess the word your partner is trying to communicate through a limited number of clues.

## What do I need to play it?

Paper, a pen and a stopwatch.

## How many friends?

Great for small groups of between four and eight pairs.

## How do I play it?

- Get yourself prepared by writing out a series of words, obscure or as obvious as you fancy making them, and fold these up and put them into a hat.

- Next, get everyone to pair up. One person from the first pair to go pulls a slip of paper out of the hat. They have to give a one-word clue (which mustn't be hyphenated or feature any part of the word that's being guessed) and their partner has five seconds to guess what the word is.

- If they can't guess what it is, the next pair is passed the word that wasn't guessed and one of them must try to communicate it by choosing another single word to give their partner a clue. Play moves around each of the pairs until the word is finally guessed, with the guessing pair scoring a point and pulling another word from the hat and starting the process over again.

- The first team to reach twenty-five wins the game.

# Cartoon Consequences

### What's the game?

This game has the potential to go off in some rather dangerous directions depending on the mood of your gathered party. Players take it in turns to write out a cartoon and caption before folding the paper and passing it on so that by the end you have an entire cartoon strip.

### What do I need to play it?

A pen and paper per player.

### How many friends?

As large or small a group as you like.

### How do I play it?

- The first player draws a cartoon and passes it to the player on his or her left, who then writes a caption below to go with it. The paper is folded down so only the caption is shown and the next player draws a cartoon that corresponds to this and folds it down so the latest cartoon is all that shows. The next player then draws a corresponding caption and so the game plays on until everyone has taken their turn.

- Once it's made its way around the table, the cartoon is opened and shared with the group.

# Drop That Phrase

## What's the game?

I used to love playing this game until my friends advised me that they'd had enough. For some reason its entertainment value seemed to last a lot longer for me. The game involves guests trying to drop their allocated phrase into conversation without being detected.

## What do I need to play it?

Some paper and a pen.

## How many friends?

Ideal for an intimate gathering of four to eight.

## How do I play it?

- To get started, write out a list of random phrases that are going to be hard to introduce into a conversation without some careful manoeuvres. You might choose something like: 'Blue bananas can be found growing in Brazil.' You need to write out one for each of the guests and distribute them discreetly and ask everyone to keep quiet about the phrase they've been given.

- The challenge is that guests must introduce their phrase into the conversation by the end of the evening without being detected. If they are detected, they are out. An incorrect detection scores the accuser a black mark; three black marks and you're also out.

- Those who manage to introduce their phrases without being detected are the winners.

# Stinky Pinky

### What's the game?

Stinky Pinky is a hilarious game that can be played out slowly throughout an evening. With a dash of creative imagination you can come up with some brilliant rhymes that will have your guests in stitches. A 'Stinky Pinky', for those who haven't already figured it out, is a smelly little finger – of course!

### What do I need to play it?

Some gathered guests, ideally with a sense of humour.

### How many friends?

Ideal for dinner parties of any size.

### How do I play it?

- The objective of Stinky Pinky is to come up with a rhyming adjective and noun for the rest of the players to guess what it is.

- Players score a point for every successful one put forward and a point goes to the person who correctly guesses what it is.

- You can either go around the table and everyone must come up with one, or have it as something that carries on throughout the evening that everyone dips in and out of. You might choose something like 'A lady's powerful night-time attire – mighty nighty' or 'An anglepoise light – camp lamp'.

- If you find you're getting good at it, you can extend the point system to award one point for one-syllable words, two points for two-syllable words and so on and so forth. The person with the most points by the end of the game is of course the winner.

# Up Jenkins

## What's the game?

Up Jenkins is a very simple Victorian game of detection that works brilliantly after dinner. It's ideal to decide who's going to do the washing-up, as the forfeit for the losing team is banishment to the kitchen sink while the winners kick back and enjoy another game.

## What do I need to play it?

A coin.

## How many friends?

A nice full table – the more the merrier.

## How do I play it?

- Split the table into two. The first team takes the coin and secretly passes it between themselves under the table, minimising movements or laying false movement clues as to the whereabouts of the coin.

- When someone on the opposing team thinks they know where the coin is, they shout 'Up Jenkins!' and point at the offending player, who must then stand up and reveal whether the coin is in their fist. If correct, the guessing team score a point. The coin is then handed over for the other team to play.

- First team to score five wins the pleasure of not doing the washing-up.

# Hand-to-Hand Combat

## What's the game?

This passing game is a more developed version of Up Jenkins. It requires a degree of dexterity and concentration and is an ideal filler between courses – or a way to persuade your group to join you in an evening of gaming fun.

## What do I need to play it?

A number of small passable objects, one for each guest.

## How many friends?

Ideal for a dinner party of any reasonable size.

## How do I play it?

- Each guest around the table is given a small passable item. Two of the items are nominated as special and everyone is made aware of which these are.

- Everyone passes most of the objects one way, except the two nominated objects which are passed in the opposite direction.

- When the game leader shouts the word 'change!' the passing direction for each object is reversed, ensuring that the two nominated objects go round in a different direction to the rest.

- Players are out as soon as they drop or fail to pass the items in the correct direction.

# Cake Race

## What's the game?

I still struggle to believe it, but this was a Victorian favourite played out in parlours throughout the period. It's hard to imagine such base and disgraceful table manners and outright gorging taking place even today, but if the Victorians approved of it, it can't be all that bad.

## What do I need to play it?

A cake cut into equal portions for each player, and something to tie everyone's hands behind their backs.

## How many friends?

However many slices of cake you have, or vice versa. Essentially, it's great for any number.

## How do I play it?

- Cut up and distribute your cake.
- Tie your dinner guests' arms behind their backs and ask them to consume their cake using only their mouths.
- If you want to take it to the Victorian finale, then the winner is the one who licks their plate, picks it up with their teeth and manages to drop it over their head behind them. I'd suggest using plastic plates to prevent an even greater mess than is necessary.

# SIX

# Raucous Organised Fun for Dinner Parties

Not all dinner parties wind up as all together civilised affairs. If you're hosting a gathering of old buddies or close family friends, what starts off as cultured conversation over aperitifs can soon descend into the banal by the time the plates are cleared.

My favourite sort of dinner parties are those that continue well into the night, with the gathered guests bonding over long hours of game playing. It's always such an accolade for the host of an evening when their guests stay up way past the sensible hour when all good people are tucked up at home in bed.

If the general mood of your gathered guests is erring away from philosophical discussions and they're seeking distractions of the more frolicsome kind, the following chapter is stacked with game ideas that will have them tittering into their coffees and rolling onto the floor.

# Fuzzy Duck

### What's the game?

A rather amusing drinking game, the sole intention of which is to get you to say a rude and rather immature spoonerism. Another student favourite that should entertain if you're in a drinking mood.

### What do I need to play it?

Some animated and well-oiled friends with drinks in their hands.

### How many friends?

Good for medium-sized groups of between six and twelve.

### How do I play it?

- Get yourself set up so you're in a sort of circular position, or can at least see and hear everyone in your group.
- Someone starts off the game by saying 'Fuzzy Duck' to the person on the left. 'Fuzzy Duck' is then repeated around the circle until someone chooses to say 'Does he?', which sends it back around in the opposite direction with everyone saying 'Ducky Fuzz' instead.
- This carries on until someone gets it wrong and they have to take a drink.

# Remember When...?

## What's the game?

This game is a novel take on charades, ideal for a gathering of close friends or a reunion of old buddies. It makes the most of the inherent pleasure of reliving shared memories as guests take it in turns to act out embarrassing and memorable episodes and anecdotes involving your group of friends.

## What do I need to play it?

A group of close friends or family with shared memories.

## How many friends?

You really need a minimum of four, with a maximum of ten or twelve.

## How do I play it?

- Before starting, each guest takes some time to recall episodes that they know the group will remember. Try to choose those that are as embarrassing as possible, so rather than bringing up when Josie got pregnant, focus more on the time she went on a first date and her beau vomited over her at the restaurant table (and yes, that did actually happen. Dave, you are forgiven). The stories can be about themselves or about another mutual friend or member of the gathering. There are bound to be a couple of obvious ones that a few people plan to do, and I'm sure there's someone in your group whose name might pop up more than once.

- When ready, guests take it in turns to act out their episode. The entertainment value of this game is normally more than enough to negate the need to add a competitive element, but if necessary you can award points for how quickly the group guesses, for example four points if they guess in under thirty seconds, three points if within a minute, two points if within ninety seconds and one point if within two minutes.

# Flight Commander Colonel Warrington Smyth

## What's the game?

This is a great memory game that's ideal to play around the dinner table at big family gatherings when all the eating is done. It involves players trying to remember the routine of actions performed by each guest as they take their turn to make a toast.

## What do I need to play it?

Players with full bellies and full glasses.

## How many friends?

As many as are sat around your table. Great for all ages.

## How do I play it?

- The game involves players taking it in turns to make a toast and performing a routine of actions that each player then adds to as their turn comes around.

- The person to open the game briefly explains the rules and announces: 'I'd like to make a toast to Flight Commander Colonel Warrington Smyth.' After the toast is made, the player takes a sip of their drink and then performs an action such as tapping their glass, knocking on the table or even doing a twist, before sitting down again.

- It's then the turn of the next player along. This player stands up, makes a toast, takes a sip of their drink, and does the action the last player did, before adding an action of their own.

- The game continues around and around the table. If a player forgets a move, they are out.

- The last player to remember the entire routine is declared the winner.

# Zoom, Schwartz, Pafigliano

### What's the game?

This is a quick-fire drinking game that requires considerable concentration. The aim is to be the last player left in after negotiating a series of word and eye movements to navigate your way to the winning line.

### What do I need to play it?

Just yourselves and a suitable forfeit, drinking or otherwise.

### How many friends?

Works best in groups of four or above.

### How do I play it?

- The aim of the game is to get the right order of eye contact and word dialogue between the group. A mistake results in a forfeit and three mistakes means you're out of the game.

- To get started, make sure everyone is crystal clear on the rules:
  - Zoom: to start the game, the first player chooses a random person and looks them in the eye and says 'Zoom'.
  - Schwartz: the person who has been Zoomed must then choose to either Zoom someone else by looking them in the eye and saying 'Zoom', or get the person back who Zoomed them in the first place by saying 'Schwartz' but not looking them in the eye.
  - Pafigliano: the person who has been Schwartzed then has the choice of looking at a new person and saying 'Zoom', or sending it right back to the person who just Schwartzed them by saying 'Pafigliano' without looking at them.
- Got it? So you can only Zoom someone new, and Schwartz and Pafigliano are for bouncing back and forth battles. In Zoom you look someone in the eyes, and with the other two you avoid eye contact.
- It sounds quite simple when put like that, but the practice is quite different.

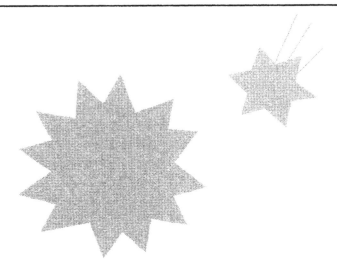

# Picture This

## What's the game?

This game is as amusing to watch as it is to play. It's fascinating to observe people's inability to communicate something very simple.

## What do I need to play it?

A stopwatch and a pillowcase filled with an eclectic collection of interestingly shaped objects, plus a pad, a pen and a blindfold for every pair you have playing.

## How many friends?

Great for an intimate dinner party of six to eight to prevent too much waiting around. Play is in pairs so you really need an even number to prevent anyone feeling left out.

## How do I play it?

- Get yourself prepared by collecting together some interesting items in a pillowcase. I'd allow about three for each pair, or more if you want the game to go on longer.

- Get everyone to pair up, blindfold one player from each of the pairs and give them each a pad and pen. Next, get one person to select an item out of the pillowcase, which is passed around the group and then left in the middle of the table.

- On the word 'Go!', the seeing partner must describe the object to their blindfolded friend. They're not allowed to say what it is or that it looks like another object; they can only describe its shape, colour and texture. The blindfolded player must draw what they think the object described looks like. Seeing players are allowed to verbally direct their partner's pens, i.e. 'to the left a bit' or 'a lovely long line' and 'stop'. Each pair has sixty seconds to complete the task

- After the sixty seconds is up, players can remove their blindfolds and everyone must vote for whose drawing they think is best, bearing in mind that you're not allowed to vote for your own. The team whose performance is voted the best scores a point.

- Pairs then swap over so that the describer is blindfolded this time and play continues.

- The first team to five points is the winner.

# Barney's Bum

## What's the game?

This game is ideal if you have a gathering of friends or family who are in a mildly obnoxious mood and fancy causing a racket while they wait for their supper.

## What do I need to play it?

Some good old-fashioned clappy hands.

## How many friends?

As many as can fit around your dinner table.

## How do I play it?

- The aim of the game is to remember which movements everyone has chosen to enable you to effectively pass the signal around the group.

- First of all, everyone needs to decide on what their movement is and communicate this to the rest of the group. It might be to touch your nose, swing your head or even to spin around; it can be as elaborate or as simple as you wish.

- To get started, get a simple and regular beat going with everyone in unison, e.g. 'clap clap' and then hands down on table 'beat, beat', repeating it over and over again.

- The first person to go stops clapping briefly while everyone else continues, performs their movement and then follows it with the movement of someone else, before joining back in with the clapping. The person whose movement has just been performed by the first player must respond by performing their movement and then the movement of someone else.

- The game continues in this way until someone messes up and needs to take a forfeit. The game then picks up again and continues on, and on, and on until you've all got bored of it. Which might take quite some time.

# Chair Chess

## What's the game?

This game is a bit like the previous game, Barney's Bum, in that people communicate to each other via signals. This time, instead of using signals to communicate messages to each other, your guests are famous singers or writers (or whatever category you wish) and are required to jump up and change places on request. This game is ideal if you fancy shaking up your dinner party by mixing up the seating arrangements and getting everyone to move around under the guise of a game.

## What do I need to play it?

Some willing and not too full dinner guests.

## How many friends?

As many as can fit around your table.

## How do I play it?

- Everyone around the table gives themselves the name of a different celebrity. The first person to go shouts out their own celebrity name and that of another guest. These two guests swap places.
- The person whose name was just called then shouts out their name and perhaps the names of three others. These four people swap places.
- The game plays on with players shouting out as high an even number of celebrity names (including their own) as they can remember, causing the named guests to change seats.
- The game plays on until everyone is exhausted from all the moving around.

# Whose Feet Are They Anyway?

## What's the game?

In this game teams try to guess whose feet, ankles or indeed knees are on display.

## What do I need to play it?

A thick blanket and somewhere to suspend it from with enough room for people to walk behind, and a well-lit room to play in. You also need a pad and pen for each player.

## How many friends?

You need to have enough of you for two teams and for the guessing to be relatively hard. The minimum is probably eight for this game.

## How do I play it?

- Get your room set up by suspending your blanket so that the tallest person will be hidden behind it with only their ankles or knees revealed. Make sure your room is bright enough to prevent people's shadows giving the game away.

- Next, get everyone into teams and ask the first team to go to the other side of the blanket and remove their shoes and socks and roll their trousers up. Issue a pad and pen to the other team.

- The team behind the blanket present their feet one by one, while the viewing team write down who they think each person is.

- Then the team behind the curtain emerge, take people's pads for marking and announce who was number 1, 2 and so on.

- Scores are totted up with each correct guess earning a point, and the teams swap places.

- The team with the highest cumulative score after both sides have played are declared the winners.

# The Card of Desire

## What's the game?

This is a really simple but fun acting game that'll give your guests a chance to show off their theatrical prowess. Players act out the depth of their desire based on the value of the card they've been issued with.

## What do I need to play it?

A pack of cards.

## How many friends?

As large or as small a group as you have gathered.

## How do I play it?

- Decide which two people are going first and get them to sit on two chairs in front of the rest of the group.

- Each must pick and conceal a card from the pack. One of those watching must shout out a scenario that the pair are in, for example, at the doctors or waving goodbye on the deck of a cruise liner.

- On the word 'Go!', the pair must get into their roles but at the same time act out the depth of their desire for each other based on the value of the cards they picked. For example, if the value of the chosen card is two, this equals zero desire. If the king has been selected, a deeply infatuated and obsessive passion needs to be acted out.

- After one minute, the rest of the guests try to guess the value of the cards. Two of the correct guessers or those that were the closest are next up.

# Never Have I Ever

## What's the game?

This is a great way to learn a bit more about your friends. We played it late one night after coming back from the pub and found out much more than we wanted about one person. He still hasn't recovered his dignity after that particular revelation.

## What do I need to play it?

A group of friends who know each other well enough to reveal some of their darker secrets. Everyone needs a place to sit as well.

## How many friends?

Great for groups of all sizes.

## How do I play it?

- One person stands in the middle with the others sat comfortably and in full view around them.

- The person in the middle needs to announce something they've never done before, for example 'I've never been to Denver'. This is a mild example in case any young eyes find their way to this book. You can of course be a bit more daring with your statements.

- Ideally, someone in the group will announce that they have been to Denver and they must get up and swap places with the person in the middle. If no one answers, the person in the middle simply makes another statement. If several people respond, the group then votes to decide who should go in the middle.

- The game plays on in this way with guests swapping and revealing. If someone is exposed as not admitting to something they have in fact done (they'll be the ones quietly sinking into the sofa), they then step into the middle.

- Let's hope you don't find out anything too shocking!

# Duct Tape Challenge

## What's the game?

This was another game associated with the days of my youth, probably because we were able to destroy the paintwork of our decrepit student houses without anyone noticing. If you're not planning on decorating any time soon, or if you have a landlord who would be markedly miffed by chunks of plaster and paint falling off the walls, then choose an unpainted exterior wall to play on.

This game is a competition to see who can stay taped to a wall the longest.

## What do I need to play it?

A roll of very strong duct tape per team and some strong, unpainted, unplastered exterior walls. You also need a stopwatch and something for the taped person to stand on – a strong box or chair, ideally not too far off the ground.

## How many friends?

Teams of however many want to play, with one person willing to be taped to the wall.

## How do I play it?

- Get everyone into teams and nominate who in each team is going to be taped to the wall.
- Stand this person on their step or chair. On the word 'Go!', teams have five minutes to tape their teammate to the wall. The aim of the game is to make the taping as strong as possible, as the person who stays up longest wins.
- Once the person is taped up, step back and watch to see how long your handiwork will stay in place. The team whose person stays taped up on the wall the longest is the winner.

# Table Sock-Wrestling

### What's the game?

You'll need to ensure your guests aren't squeamish about fondling each other's feet. And you might want to have some clean socks to hand in case of any offensively dirty guests. This game involves a foot-to-foot battle to try to remove each other's socks.

### What do I need to play it?

Some clean socks for each player. Make sure they're of the same elasticity and of the appropriate size for each wearer to prevent accusations of unfair advantage. The looser the socks are the better, otherwise matches can go on for quite a long time and can even get a little bit violent as time goes on.

### How many friends?

However many pairs are up for playing.

### How do I play it?

- Depending on how much room and how many players you have, it's probably best to run this as a tournament with pairs competing and the winners making it through to the qualifying rounds.

- Get your first playing pair to face each other with their toes connecting. If you've got a lot of people, you might want to play multiple matches at the same time.

- On the word 'Go!', players must attempt to remove each other's socks using only their own feet.

- The first player to remove their opponent's socks wins.

- Winners then go on to play other winners until an ultimate champion is identified.

# Toe Wrestling

## What's the game?

Toe Wrestling has been growing in popularity since its emergence in Staffordshire in the 1990s. Two walkers who stopped off at a pub while on a long hike devised the event. They were keen to invent an Olympic sport that the Brits could win. The landlord at Ye Olde Royal Oak Inn in Wetton was keen to support the pioneers in their mission and in 1993 launched the World Toe Wrestling Championships.

The sport is much like Arm Wrestling. Players compete to wrestle each other off the Toedium.

## What do I need to play it?

Strong ankles, clean feet, and something to make the Toedium (a large book will do).

## How many friends?

A party-load of you.

## How do I play it?

- Contestants sit themselves down opposite each other and place their feet on the Toedium with their big toes interlocking.
- On the word 'Go!', they wrestle with each other to get their competitor's foot off the Toedium. Players then swap over to the other foot and do the same, before returning to the first foot to complete the best-of-three knockout competition.

# Hairbrush Dramatics

### What's the game?

If you have a gregarious bunch of friends with theatrical leanings, this game will give them the chance to showcase their talents. Teams are challenged to perform a sketch utilising a variety of household items.

### What do I need to play it?

A bag filled with up to ten household bits and pieces per team. Include a wide range of items, the more random and bizarre the better. You'll also need a stopwatch.

### How many friends?

Great for large groups.

### How do I play it?

- Get everyone into teams and issue them with their collection of items. Each team then has ten minutes to go away and prepare a sketch that will utilise every household item in some way or other (hint: a banana isn't always a piece of fruit; it can also make a very handy telephone) and must include every person in the group.

- Groups then take it in turns to perform their sketch and guests vote for the winner.

# Elves, Gnomes and Giants

## What's the game?

This game will appeal to *Lord of the Rings* fans. It involves a live but non-contact duel between the Elves, Gnomes and Giants. Great to resolve any squabbles and burn off any unwanted testosterone.

## What do I need to play it?

Nothing – just some friends ready for battle.

## How many friends?

A minimum of six and a maximum of however many fit in the room.

## How do I play it?

- Split everyone into two teams. The aim of the game is to defeat the opposite team following similar rules to Paper, Scissors, Stone, but this time Elves beat Gnomes, Giants beat Elves, and Gnomes beat Giants.

- Get each team positioned at opposite ends of the room, huddled together deciding what they're going to be: Elves, Gnomes or Giants. On the word 'Go!', players charge towards each other displaying the gestures and body language of their adopted beast and shouting out what they all are.

- Whichever team wins scores a point and the game plays on. If both teams choose to be the same beast, it's a draw and they stay in the middle and must decide in whispers what they're going to be.

- First team to win three rounds are the winners.

# The Camera Game

## What's the game?

If you fancy getting some novel pictures to remind yourself of your evening of organised fun, then this game delivers. Players pass a camera around the table as quickly as possible to avoid the self-timer going off when it's in their hands.

## What do I need to play it?

A camera with a self-timer facility.

## How many friends?

As many as are sat around your dinner table.

## How do I play it?

- Set your camera to self-timer. As soon as the timer's on, pass the camera around the table. Whoever has the camera when the self-timer goes off is out. The camera is then reset and passed around again.
- The last person left in is the winner.

# Fungal Bum Candle

## What's the game?

This is a hilarious game that I was introduced to by my lovely friends Hannah and Louis. The basic idea is to put out a candle positioned between your legs by swinging and lowering a piece of fungus that is suspended from your trousers on string. Simples.

## What do I need to play it?

Each player will need a tea-light, a jam jar, a mushroom and a half-metre of string. Players also need to be wearing trousers with belt loops.

## How many friends?

As many as are prepared to play.

## How do I play it?

- First of all, get yourselves set up by tying one end of the string to the mushroom and the other end to the belt loop at the back of your trousers. Next, position yourselves astride a lit tea-light with the mushroom dangling majestically between your legs.

- On the word 'Go!', race to put out the flame using the mushroom. The first player to achieve the task is the winner.

# Animal-Lovers

### What's the game?

This was another popular game at university. I seemed to have a penchant for games that involved animal noises at the time – I'm not sure what that was about. Anyway, the aim of the game is to find your animal-lover among the cacophony of sounds emitting from the gathered guests.

### What do I need to play it?

Paper and pens. A mastery of animal impressions is an advantage.

### How many friends?

A minimum of six. The larger the group the better, but you need to have an even number.

### How do I play it?

- The aim of this game is to identify your animal partner from the symphony of animal sounds emitted from the gathered guests.

- To get yourself set up, you need to write out two slips of paper for every animal and there needs to be a slip of paper for every guest. Fold these up, pop them in a hat and get everyone to pick one out.

- On the word 'Go!', guests need to start behaving like their allocated animal, preferably making its mating cry, while keeping their ears and eyes tuned for their animal partner.

- The last pair to find each other are the losers.

# Ace Heads and Tails Game

## What's the game?

This is a brilliant game invented by my friend Andy. It's a winner for large groups, teasing everyone into an evening of homespun fun. Put simply (well, it's hard to complicate it as it is indeed a simple game), the game involves a slow process of elimination by the toss of a coin.

## What do I need to play it?

A large group of friends and a coin for flicking.

## How many friends?

As many as you can muster. This one's great for large groups.

## How do I play it?

- Get everyone to stand up and decide whether to put their hands on their heads or their tails (i.e. their bums).
- Toss a coin and whatever it lands on determines who stays standing up, i.e. if it lands on tails, all of those with their hands on their heads have to sit down.
- This process of elimination continues until you are left with a winner (or two).

# Ibble Dibble

### What's the game?

Ideal for wine-soaked late-night sessions. It leaves you covered in sooty spots, but it will certainly provoke some giggles.

### What do I need to play it?

Everyone definitely needs a drink for this game. You'll also need a couple of corks and a lighter, and some friends with a sense of humour.

### How many friends?

Ideal for a late-night dinner-party gathering.

### How do I play it?

- Give everyone around the table a number. The aim of the game is to coherently announce yourself and the number of sooty spots you have on your face and hand over to another member of the group by announcing them and their number of sooty spots.

- An Ibble Dibble is a player, so for example I might be Number One Ibble Dibble, and the sooty spots on the player's face are called Dibble Ibbles.

- So to get started, char the end of the cork (making sure it's not still hot by the time you come to use it). The first person in the group to go says 'This is Number One Ibble Dibble with no Dibble Ibbles calling Number Three Ibble Dibble with no Dibble Ibbles'. Number Three Ibble Dibble would then respond in the same way, calling someone else in the group.

- As soon as a player makes a mistake, they take a drink and are marked with the cork, leaving a sooty black spot – a Dibble Ibble.

- This game gets harder and more ridiculous as play goes on. One to avoid if you're planning on heading out anywhere afterwards.

# Touching the Blarney Stone

## What's the game?

There are a whole host of theories surrounding the history and cultural significance of the Blarney Stone. Some say it's Jacob's pillow; others say it was the stone that Moses struck to produce water for the Israelites. While the provenance of these theories is uncertain, the popular activity of giving the stone a slobbery kiss is an essential element of the many pilgrimages visitors from across the world make to Ireland.

In this game, players stumble around the room with their eyes closed and arms outstretched in search of the sacred Blarney.

## What do I need to play it?

Some willing guests.

## How many friends?

As large a group as you have gathered.

## How do I play it?

- Ask your guests to stand up and walk around the room with their eyes closed. I'd get them to keep their heads dropped with their chins on their chests to prevent any unfair cheating.

- The game leader then steps forward and taps someone on the shoulder, and they become the Blarney Stone. This person must remain stock still.

- The rest of the group walk around with their arms outstretched and every time they bump into someone they must ask, 'Blarney?' If that person is not the Blarney Stone, they of course say 'No'.

- When a player bumps into the Blarney Stone and asks, 'Blarney?' the Blarney Stone must remain silent and the other player then opens their eyes and continues to stand beside him, while silently touching him.

- The game continues in this way until there is one player left looking for the Blarney Stone. This person is the loser.

# The Sofa Game

## What's the game?

The Sofa Game was an illicit game we used to play as teenagers that allowed everyone to get their first kiss. It involved the girls sitting on the sofa and the boys lining up and taking it in turns to give us a slobbery one. If you liked someone then rather than just a quick peck on the cheek, you hung about a bit longer.

Feel free to roll out the above version at will, but this format is all about the males and females competing to get all the members of their gender on the sofa. Ideal for when your guests fancy getting away from the table and kicking back somewhere more comfortable.

## What do I need to play it?

A large sofa and a collection of chairs.

## How many friends?

As many friends as you have seats. You need one extra seat for the number of players playing e.g. if you have a four-seated sofa, you'll need five chairs for eight of you to play. You also need an equal number of males and females.

## How do I play it?

- Write everyone's names onto slips of paper, fold them up and put them in a hat. Everyone picks out a name. Whoever they pick, this is the person they must be throughout the game. It's important that they don't disclose this to anyone else.

- Get your sofas and chairs set up in a circular shape and get everyone sat down alternating between boy and girl, leaving the extra chair left empty.

- The aim of the game is to get everyone of the same sex onto the sofa.
- The person sat to the right of the empty chair shouts out someone's name in the hope of removing someone from the sofa into the chair. The person whose name is called (well, pretend name for the game) moves from wherever they're sat into the empty chair, leaving their place empty.
- The person sat to the right of the newly empty seat does the same and so the game plays on.
- The trick of the game is to try to remember what everyone's pseudonym is with the aim of manoeuvring their gender onto the sofa. Whichever gender gets all of its members onto the sofas first wins.

# Flexible Friends

## What's the game?

This game is a novel take on Twister and can be played without that big plastic sheet. It's ideal for yoga-loving or freewheeling flexible friends who are up for getting themselves into a bit of a contortionist's pickle.

## What do I need to play it?

You need paper, pens and a die.

## How many friends?

Two to eight ideally, to prevent too much waiting around.

## How do I play it?

- Write out sheets of paper with numbers one to six on them and scatter these around the room at distances that stretched-out limbs will be able to reach.

- The first player to go throws the dice and puts one foot on the number rolled. The other players follow suit by each rolling the dice and positioning a foot on the number they roll.

- In the next round, players put their other foot on the next number rolled. Then in the third and fourth rounds they must use their hands.

- When a player falls over, they are out. Last player still standing is the winner.

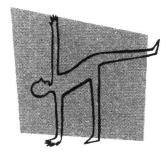

# Look of the Season

### What's the game?

This one's perfect for aspiring fashion designers or anyone with a bit of creative flair. It was born out of a birthday weekend in a thatched cottage in the countryside. It culminated in a fully commentated fashion show, with all of us wearing the winner's new designs for the rest of the evening.

### What do I need to play it?

Whatever you can lay your hands on – bin bags, kitchen roll, curtains, sheets, bath mat, feather duster – you get the idea.

### How many friends?

As many teams as you like. I'd suggest no more than four players in each team.

### How do I play it?

- Players get into teams and are given a set amount of time to go away and design an outfit from whatever they can lay their hands on.
- The only rule is that actual clothing is banned. Outfits need to be customised from whatever can be found around the house. You can choose to have one model with the rest of the group creating, or you might opt to have the whole team wearing a collection of the inspired creations.
- Points should be awarded for creativity and inspired accessorising.

# Human Buckaroo

## What's the game?

This game can only be played when someone in your party has dozed off. They need to be pretty sound asleep – or drunk – to ensure they're not woken by the lightest of touches.

Remember the 1980s game Buckaroo? Well, this is the real-life version.

## What do I need to play it?

A large stack of empty plastic cups and a sleeping guest.

## How many friends?

At least two of you to play, and one sleeping victim.

## How do I play it?

- Once you're certain that your victim is fast asleep, players each take a plastic cup and take it in turns to gently balance them somewhere on the sleeper. This must be done extremely carefully as the object of the game is not to wake up the victim.
- Whoever has just positioned their cup when the sleeper awakes is the loser.

# Fizz Buzz

## What's the game?

You might argue on first read that this one should be confined to the maths class. Strangely, it is brilliant to play with friends and only requires a very basic grasp of the times table.

## What do I need to play it?

Some sort of forfeit device, if you decide to play with forfeits. This is probably best known as a drinking game, but you could use a points system instead, where points are awarded for each mess-up and chores assigned to the person with the most. Alternatively, come up with some embarrassing things that players have to do, for example swapping clothes with the person sat opposite or trying to sing a song while gargling water.

## How many friends?

You could play it with two of you, but great to play in a medium-sized group.

## How do I play it?

- Get everyone to sit in a circle and then take it in turns to count, so the first player would say 'One', the next would say 'Two', and so on.
- When a player gets to a number that is divisible by three they must say, 'Fizz', and when they reach one that's divisible by five they must say, 'Buzz', so, for example: 'One', 'Two', 'Fizz', 'Four', 'Buzz', 'Fizz' . . .
- If playing with points, everyone starts with five and then loses one each time they get it wrong until they have no points left and they're out. Alternatively, you can use drinks as forfeits for mathematical errors.

# SEVEN

# Organised Fun for Celebrations and Events

Most of us had our first brush with organised fun at childhood birthday parties. From jigging up and down to music around a line of chairs to hungrily watching a parcel being passed among our friends, you could always expect a few favourites to make their appearance on any children's-party itinerary. It's because of the predictable presence of certain games at these colourful occasions that we file them away as 'kids' stuff', rather than reviewing their fun potential and rolling them out again as get older.

Some of the best parties I've been to are the ones where we've reinstated and rejuvenated many of these old classics. There's nothing that will shake the hipsters off their posing podiums or drag the wallflowers from their pots more than a classic party game with a modern, grown-up twist.

If you fancy rediscovering the joys of childhood festivities, then this chapter bursts with new twists on the old classics and a few downright daft ideas for fun.

# Musical Lap Dancing

## What's the game?

This is a great way to spice up the traditional game of Musical Chairs and to encourage some intimate frolicking at a party.

## What do I need to play it?

Some music.

## How many friends?

A party-load of you.

## How do I play it?

- Count how many players you have, divide this in two and take one off: this is how many chairs you need to line up in a row. Position them in two rows back to back if there are a lot of you playing.
- Put the music on and get everyone dancing around. This time, when the music stops, players must race to sit down or sit on someone's lap.
- The last pair left standing are sadly the losers.

# Musical Chairs

## What's the game?

We've had many a party where the coolest
members of the group have been found
holding out until the bitter 'shove your mate
off the last chair' end in a game of Musical
Chairs. For those not familiar with the game,
it involves dancing around an ever-decreasing
number of chairs and dashing to sit down
when the music stops.

## What do I need to play it?

A lot of chairs and a stereo or something to make the music.

## How many friends?

Brilliant for a huge group, but it will obviously depend on how
many chairs you've got.

## How do I play it?

- First of all, line up two rows of chairs back to back down the middle of the room. You need a big playing space, so clear the other furniture out of the way. You also need to ensure that there are enough chairs minus one for everyone playing the game. If there are a few of you and it's after dinner, you can use your dinner table as the set-up. Just make sure you've properly cleared the table to prevent glasses or plates getting smashed.

- Put the music on and get everyone to dance around the chairs. To make sure there's no aggressive chair-coveting, people need to keep moving around as they dance.

- At a point when people least expect it, turn the music off. Players must dash to a chair and sit down on it. The last person to do this is out. No lap-sitting is allowed.

- Before putting the music back on, move one chair out of the field of play.

- The game continues in the same format until there's one chair and two people left. The first to sit down when the music stops wins.

# Blindfolded Musical Chairs

## What's the game?

This is exactly the same as a standard game of Musical Chairs, but this time players are blindfolded and need to fumble towards their chair destination. Last one in is the winner.

# Rockers, Ravers and Disco Divas Musical Statues

### What's the game?

Shake up the traditional game of Musical Statues by getting everyone to do their favourite dance moves, making sure they're showing their best Rocker, Raver or Disco Diva shape by the time the music stops.

### What do I need to play it?

Some music.

### How many friends?

A big fat party of you.

### How do I play it?

- Pop the music on and get everyone dancing around. When the music stops, everyone must choose to throw down their preferred Rocker, Raver or Disco dance move.

- The first person to move is out. Last person in is the winner.

# Human Musical Chairs

## What's the game?

If getting hold of chairs is a bit of a struggle, this alternative makes use of humans instead. In this format the men become the chairs for the ladies to elegantly sit on.

## What do I need to play it?

Some music.

## How many friends?

A party-load of you.

## How do I play it?

- Make sure that you have an even number of players of both genders and get the music going and everyone dancing around.
- When the music stops the men need to get down on their hands and knees and the ladies need to sit on their backs. Last couple to get seated are out.
- The other rule with this game is that players aren't allowed to sit on the back of someone they've already sat on.
- Last pair left in are the winners.

# Synchronised Statues

### What's the game?

Synchronised Statues is an excellent twist on the normal game of Musical Statues, ideal for the disco divas and podium dancers among your gathered friends. Couples execute elaborate synchronised dancing manoeuvres that only take place from the waist up.

### What do I need to play it?

Some music.

### How many friends?

Great for big groups. You'll need an even number of players.

### How do I play it?

- Get everyone paired up and put the music on.
- Players must mirror each other's dance moves – the more elaborate the better. When the music stops they must freeze and hold position. If someone moves, that couple is out.
- Last couple left in are the winners.

# The Dancing Game

## What's the game?

This is yet another game that came out of our fun-packed university years. It reached its peak when half a nightclub joined in, at a temple to Bristol hedonism known as Lakota. It used to have a fantastic balcony that overlooked the dance floor, where some friends and I managed to engage everyone in a session of mass organised fun. Since then it's been rolled out on many an occasion and is a brilliant way to get reluctant dancers to hit the floor. Persevere with this one and it'll be worth it.

## What do I need to play it?

Some willing dancers.

## How many friends?

You could play it with just two of you, but definitely the more the better.

## How do I play it?

- Get everyone to stand in a circle, or at least in a position where you can all see each other.
- The first person starts by doing a dance move – think John Travolta in *Saturday Night Fever*. The next person then leads the rest of the players to copy the first move, before adding a move of their own. To help people remember the sequence, it's useful to shout out a description of each move as it comes up.
- And so the game plays on, with each player adding a move until you've put together an entire routine that continues to grow and grow.

# Fancy-Dress Pass the Parcel

## What's the game?

If you fancy making your friends look a little bit silly, then this game will be right up your boulevard. Same rules as for Pass the Parcel, but for this one every time the music stops, the player holding the parcel has to take an item of clothing out of a bag and put it on.

## What do I need to play it?

Get a sack, bin liner or lightweight bag and fill it full of lots of different items of clothing, the funnier the better. Think stupid wigs or the collection of bad-taste 1980s clothing hidden at the back of your wardrobe and you'll get the general idea. You'll also need a stereo to play some music to accompany the passing.

## How many friends?

Great for large groups.

## How do I play it?

- Collect your dressing-up clothes together and put them in a bag.
- Get everyone up and dancing around and tossing the present around in the air between them while the music is playing.
- When the music stops, the person holding the bag has to reach in, pull out an item and put it on.
- The music then starts again and the game continues.
- The person who puts the last item on is the winner.

# Knights, Horses and Cavaliers

## What's the game?

This is an ace alternative to Musical Statues.

## What do I need to play it?

Nothing.

## How many friends?

Ideally an equal pairing of males and females in the group, plus a facilitator.

## How do I play it?

- Get your young friends to pair up, ideally with someone from the opposite sex.
- When the music's on, the pairs must prance and dance around at will. When the music stops, the facilitator shouts either 'Knight!', 'Horse!' or 'Cavalier!'
- 'Knight!' means the man has to give his partner a piggyback, 'Horse!' means the man has to give their partner a horse ride by getting on all fours, and 'Cavalier!' means the male has to get down on one knee and the woman sits on the knee that's uppermost.
- The last couple to execute the manoeuvre is out, and so the game plays on until the remaining couple are announced the winners.

# Balloon Bashing

## What's the game?

If your gathered guests are in an energetic mood and up for bashing each other about a bit, this one will go down a treat.

## What do I need to play it?

A balloon on a string and a rolled-up newspaper per player.

## How many friends?

However many you have to hand.

## How do I play it?

- Blow up the balloons, attach the strings and get your guests to tie them to their ankles. Each person should also have a rolled-up newspaper.
- On the word 'Go!', they must chase each other around, bashing others' balloons with the rolled-up newspaper to make them burst.
- Last person left with an intact balloon is declared the winner.

# The Game of the Triffids

## What's the game?
It's a bit like Twister but requires more thought.

## What do I need to play it?
At least five people for the game to be effective.

## How many friends?
However many you can get your hands on, plus someone to lead the game. Alternatively, you can split into teams to make it more competitive, but it is very funny if there are lots of you.

## How do I play it?
- Teams compete to make a monster with varying numbers of limbs that touch the floor.
- Ask someone to be the non-playing game leader, as you need a person up front to shout instructions. Get everyone else into teams of at least five. If you're playing in a small group, lose the team element and just get players to play in one group.
- The game leader then briefs the players that each team is to create a monster with a varying number of legs and arms touching the ground. If, for example, there are six players, the host might ask for a monster with nine legs and five arms.
- The teams then have to create such a monster by putting the said number of limbs on the floor, while all still somehow remaining connected to each other.
- Start with a higher number of limbs to get the teams used to balancing, then slowly decrease the number as they get better.
- Whoever's leading the game needs to have their wits about them and be able to do basic maths on the hoof.
- A point is awarded at the end of each round to the team that is quickest to form the monster with the correct number of limbs in contact with the ground while still remaining in contact with each other.

# Pin the Kiss on the Poster

## What's the game?

This is another adaptation of a kids' game that's great fun for adults as well. There's a particular pleasure to be derived from watching your puckered-up uncle stagger towards a picture of his favourite politician and attempt to plant a kiss on his lips.

## What do I need to play it?

Some full-fat Marilyn Monroe red lipstick, and a poster or picture from a magazine of your selected idol or figure of dislike.

## How many friends?

Any more than six and the game loses its momentum. Smaller groups are much better.

## How do I play it?

- First of all, hang the picture of your idol at kissing height for the players.
- Next, players take it in turns to layer on a good coating of lipstick and put on the blindfold.
- When ready, the player is spun around several times to create a sense of disorientation and is then gently propelled towards the poster.
- The object of the game is for players to attempt to kiss the idol's lips. Every time a kiss is planted, you write the player's name alongside so you know whose kiss it is.
- The kiss closest to the lips wins.

# The Cornflake Heron

## What's the game?

This game will appeal to yoga-lovers as it allows guests to demonstrate their dexterity and balance. It's brilliant to watch and you might be surprised by the suppleness of some people in your group.

## What do I need to play it?

An empty cereal carton.

## How many friends?

As many as want to play it.

## How do I play it?

- The aim of the game is to demonstrate flexibility by bending down and picking up a cereal packet using only the teeth as it gets further and further away.
- Get everybody to stand in a circle. Each player takes it in turns to step forward, bend down and retrieve the cereal packet with their teeth. The rules are that no body part other than the player's feet are allowed to touch the floor, and no other object must be used for balance.
- If players fail after two goes, they're out. If you want to be strict about it, you can make it one go.
- Once the remaining players have completed the task, you then need to trim the top layer off the cereal packet by about five centimetres. You then go around the circle again, with each player attempting to pick it up with their teeth within two goes.
- The game plays on, with the box getting lower and lower as more is cut off at the end of each round and more and more players dropping out, until the last man standing is declared the winner.

# Cracker Whacker

## What's the game?

This is a rather kooky Victorian invention. This time you each tie six cream crackers to your forehead with a ribbon and then bash each other about the head with rolled-up newspapers until there's not a crumb left. I suppose those Victorians were fortunate enough to have maids and servants to clear up after them. Lucky them. We were still finding crumbs down the back of the sofa, in the drawers, under the bed and behind the toilet months afterwards. Not for the fastidiously tidy.

## What do I need to play it?

Six crackers, a thick piece of ribbon and a rolled-up newspaper per player. You need to ensure your whackers are the same size for each player to ensure that no one has an unfair advantage.

## How many friends?

As many friends as you like. Bear in mind the maths when it comes to clearing up. You're going to be left with the remnants of six cream crackers multiplied by however many friends you have playing.

## How do I play it?

- Distribute the cream crackers to ensure each player has six and then help each other to tie them to your heads with a ribbon.

- You can tie them as a stack where you're happiest to get hit, such as on the back of your head, but you do run the risk of an unseen attack from behind. You need to be sure they're firmly held in place so they don't slip out. Alternatively, it can be easier to tie a ribbon around your head and then slip the crackers in all around the ribbon. It's up to you which strategy you decide on.

- On the word 'Go!', players chase each other around the room with rolled-up newspapers and try to whack each other's crackers until they're all shattered into crumbs.
- The last person with a whole cream cracker left tied to their head after all the bashing wins.

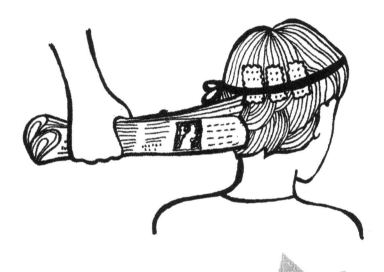

# Toilet-Paper Mummies

## What's the game?

I'm not quite sure what its appeal is, but this is one of my favourites. It sounds ridiculous when described, but bear with me and give it a go. We've played it on New Year's Eve when it's gone down a storm, but it can be a bit of a damp squib when guests aren't at the jovial, genial stage of the evening. For those conscious of wasting valuable resources, you can wind your toilet roll back up for use, but be warned: you are left with an inelegant pile of unhygienic bottom-wiping material.

## What do I need to play it?

Toilet rolls. One for each team.

## How many friends?

As many teams as you like, though ideally no more than three people in each.

## How do I play it?

- Split players into teams of three and give each team a toilet roll.

- Decide who's going to be the Egyptian mummy in each team and stand them in the middle between the other two players. Those two players then wrap the third in toilet roll by winding it around them so that they look like a mummy. If the toilet roll breaks, they must tuck the broken end in and carry on.

- The idea is to see who can create the best Toilet Paper Mummy in one minute. Judging is by the game's leader or through a group vote. Make sure you tidy the toilet paper into a bag after you've used it to save wasting resources.

- The winning team is the one who completes the task first.

# The Matchbox Gender Test

## What's the game?

This is a task that is only achievable by women. It provides much amusement as you watch the boys trying to crack it.

## What do I need to play it?

A matchbox.

## How many friends?

At least one male and one female.

## How do I play it?

- Get the first player to kneel down with heels and ankles together and palms placed flat on the floor.
- Now get someone to place the matchbox long side up so that it's positioned half a metre in front of your knees.
- Once set, sit up so your back's straight and your knees are still on the floor and clasp your hands behind your back and bend over and attempt to knock the matchbox over with your nose.
- The theory is that women find it relatively easy, but it's impossible for men to achieve.

# EIGHT

# Organised Fun for Long Journeys

Long journeys are often seen as the part of the holiday that must be endured, the penance for the indulgence of giving yourself some time off. But with some positive reframing and a raft of good ideas, the journey can become as much fun as the holiday itself.

The following chapter is jam-packed with ideas for helping you make the time you're stuck in the car, bus, train or plane scoot by. You'll be there before you know it.

# Sing-Song Ping-Pong

## What's the game?

This is a well-worn game that's entertained us for many a mile. I've included it in the car section as the acoustics produced when sitting in a metal container can be pretty impressive.

This game has nothing to do with singing talents. As my friends would delight in telling you, I very rarely sing in key. But such trivial details don't hold me back from belting out a tune with gusto.

## What do I need to play it?

Your singing voices – good or otherwise – and a pen and paper to keep the score.

## How many friends?

Ideal for two to four as it gets harder with any more.

## How do I play it?

- Decide who's going first. That person sings a line from a song.

- The rest of the group must then think of another song that features any of the words that have just been sung. For example, if I was to sing, 'Golden brown, texture like sun,' the rest of the group would have to find another song that featured any of those words, for example, 'Don't let the sun go down on me,' then perhaps followed with the next person singing, 'Things will be great when you're downtown'. I'm sure you get the idea.

- Players score a point each time they correctly sing a connecting line. I'd suggest having a nominated person to keep a track of scores; it's impossible to do when you're racking your brain for song lines.

# Sing Your Way through the Alphabet

### What's the game?

This one's an adaptation of the above game, but instead of matching a word, you have to sing songs whose titles work through the alphabet. You might start with 'Away in a Manger', for example, before moving on to 'Blowin' in the Wind'. Points awarded, as before, each time the player comes up with the next sequential song.

# Do You Know Who I Am?

## What's the game?

This is a lovely game to play in a car and one that encourages everyone to join in. Players take it in turns to guess what identity they've been given, based on the questions being asked by the other passengers.

## What do I need to play it?

Just your good selves.

## How many friends?

A car full.

## How do I play it?

- The first person to go covers their ears, while the rest of the passengers whisper to decide who this person is going to be.

- When it's agreed, get them to uncover their ears and the rest of the passengers ask him or her a series of questions subtly laden with clues about who they are. If, for example, the person was Alice in Wonderland, the questions might be 'What's the most interesting tea party you've been to?' or 'What was it like being really tall?' The clues might seem rather obvious, but for the person in the dark it can be very confusing!

- Once the player has guessed who they are, the person who asked the last question then covers their ears while their identity is agreed, and the game plays on.

# Mousehole

## What's the game?

For those familiar with the Radio 4 show *I'm Sorry I Haven't a Clue*, the game Mornington Crescent requires little introduction. Mornington Crescent is a feature of the show famous for its incredibly complicated rules. It's believed to have been invented by the panel as a way to fox an unpopular producer, as the rules are never fully explained and leave outsiders befuddled and bemused. Even to this day, the panel are still introducing new rules and caveats each time it's played.

I recently came across an old book on parlour games and found the game of Mornington Crescent described as follows, with Mousehole as an alternative title. Whether these are its true origins I'm not entirely sure, but there are indeed some minor similarities. Either way, this game lacks the complexities of the Radio 4 version and should provide some entertainment for a good hour.

Mousehole is a Victorian parlour game where players take it in turns to pick a place name, and the next player must respond by nominating another place name that starts with the letter the previous one ended with.

## What do I need to play it?

Just yourselves, and a pad and pen to keep score.

## How many friends?

A car full.

## How do I play it?

- The aim of the game is to respond to a player calling out a British town with another town starting with the letter the previous one ended in, for example, Derby, York, Kettering and so on.

- Players must avoid choosing a place which ends in M, such as Cobham, as this would allow the next player to say 'Mousehole!' and therefore win.

- It's good to choose town names where the spelling is slightly difficult, as this may hoodwink fellow players into getting their response wrong.

- If a player does get it wrong, they are out. The winner is either the last one left, or the first to be able to say 'Mousehole!'

- You can change the category used for the game. For example, it might be stations on the Underground, capital cities around the world, or something else that's relevant to you.

# Get Lost

## What's the game?

This is one to play when you've got some time on your hands, and definitely not when you're setting off with a clear destination in mind. It quite simply involves writing out some farcical directions and following them to see where they take you. The best destination wins. Oh, and you need to be in a place where none of you know your way around for it to work properly.

A friend and I came up with the game when we were travelling in India, and it was undoubtedly the making of the trip. We'd hired one of those old Enfield motorbikes and decided to head off the well-worn traveller track to escape the harassing hawkers and braying gap-year students. For a whole week, we took it in turns to write out the directions for the day and set off through rice fields, past spice farms and into rural villages, where our arrival was met with a mixture of trepidation and delight. Each afternoon we'd stop the game in the first village we came to and pay a few rupees to sleep on a family's floor for the night. My friend won the game when he managed to guide us down a rutted track and into the yard of a rural family home. The hospitality we received that day is something I'll always remember. They slaughtered one of their goats and prepared a feast that went on well into the night, with the gathered goat herders teaching us their local dance.

## What do I need to play it?

Pen and paper, a car and some time on your hands.

## How many friends?

Works brilliantly with two of you, or however many of you are in the car.

## How do I play it?

- Each person writes out a set of made-up directions, for example: 'Second left, first right . . .' and so on. Don't be too specific: avoid saying things like 'right at the roundabout' or 'left at the church', as you'd be overly lucky if these features were to appear at the right time.

- Follow the directions, and the one who set out the route to the best destination wins.

# Pub Cricket

### What's the game?

This game is ideal if you're driving around country roads in Britain, as it requires you to spot that very British thing: a country pub.

### What do I need to play it?

A car journey on some country roads.

### How many friends?

A car full. You're mildly disadvantaged if you're sat in the middle, away from the windows.

### How do I play it?

- Players take it in turns to go into bat.
- If they pass a pub while they're in play, they get a point for every leg on the pub sign. The Black Dog, for example, would earn you four points, whereas The Griffin would only score two. The highest score I know of was when Barney's cousin Tom spotted a pub called The Grand Old Duke of York. The duke and his 10,000 men scored him 22,000 points in one hit.
- Your innings ends when you pass a pub that doesn't feature any legs, for example The Star and Garter. Play then passes to the next person.
- The game stops at the end of the journey and the person with the highest score wins.

# Thumb Wars

## What's the game?

Popular in school playgrounds across Britain, this one retains its fun value for adults. Cars are a good place to play, as the confined space will stop the game getting out of hand. It's good for deciding who's going to do something, such as who's buying coffees at the next pit stop.

## What do I need to play it?

Strong thumbs.

## How many friends?

Two play at a time, but run it as a tournament if there are more of you in the car. The driver is most definitely excluded from this one.

## How do I play it?

- Face your opponent and hook all fingers of one hand with your opponent's, leaving the thumb pointing upwards as if you're doing a thumbs-up.

- Next, move your thumbs over and under each other's, while still remaining linked by your fingers, and repeat the following rhyme:
  *One, two, three, four,*
  *I declare a thumb war.*

- After the word 'war', players must battle to be the first one to squash their opponent's thumb by pushing and holding it down with theirs for three seconds.

- The thumb-squashing player is the winner.

# The Kevin Bacon Game

## What's the game?

This game works if you're a film buff and also know your celebrities. If you're good at it, it can make a six-hour journey fly by. The basic theory behind the game is that all actors can be linked to the omnipresent Kevin Bacon via the films they have worked on with him. You don't have to use Kevin Bacon, but you need someone who's been in lots of movies and very few actors have been in as many as him. Julia Roberts, Brad Pitt, Reese Witherspoon or Jack Nicholson are all fairly prolific alternatives.

The game is a variation on the Six Degrees of Separation theory – the idea that, if everyone is one step away from each person they know, then they are two steps away from the friends of that person. With this in mind, everyone is then no more than six steps away from each person on earth.

## What do I need to play it?

A good knowledge of film and Hollywood actors.

## How many friends?

Between two and four is perfect.

## How do I play it?

- The first player suggests the name of an actor or actress. Players then work all together, on their own or in pairs to figure out how that person can be linked to Kevin Bacon in as few steps as possible.

- An example that Kevin Bacon himself put forward in a book on the game is as follows: Kevin Bacon was in *Flatliners* with Julia Roberts, who was in *Closer* with Jude Law, who was in *The Talented Mr Ripley* with Gwyneth Paltrow, who was in *Seven* with Morgan Freeman, who was in *The Sum of All Fears* with Sir Alan Bates. So there are five degrees of separation between Kevin Bacon and Sir Alan Bates.

# Double Back

## What's the game?

Another one to convert motorway mundanity into a playground of verbal fun. A working knowledge of *Hello!* magazine or similar titles will give you a definite advantage.

## What do I need to play it?

A sound knowledge of famous or infamous people.

## How many friends?

Works really well with between two and eight people.

## How do I play it?

- The object of the game is to come up with famous names that start with the first letter of the surname the previous person has uttered.

- You can vary the rules to state that players must only choose living actors, or you might choose to let anarchy reign and allow any individual to be named, famous or non-famous, fictional or real. I'd recommend you have a time limit on each person's go. We normally allow ten seconds.

- The first person to go says an actor's or character's name.

- The next person must find a name that starts with the same letter as the surname of the previously mentioned character. For example, if I were to mention Simon Cowell, the next player must choose a name that begins with C, such as Carol Vorderman.

- Or you can try to come up with a character whose first name and surname start with the same letter: for example, if the previous name ended in an M, you could choose Marilyn Monroe. This sends the game back in the other direction.

- A character can only be mentioned once.

- If you mess up, i.e. if you fail to come up with a famous name within the agreed timeframe, you're out.

- Last player in wins.

# Just a Minute

## What's the game?

Just like its famous Radio 4 namesake, this game requires players to keep talking about a subject for sixty seconds. The game was invented by Ian Messiter when riding on the top deck of the number 13 bus. He remembered being petrified at being asked by one of his schoolmasters to talk non-stop for one minute and immediately recognised its entertainment potential if played with erudite and articulate friends.

## What do I need to play it?

Some sharp-talking wits about you.

## How many friends?

Two to six is best.

## How do I play it?

- All players write down five topics of conversation, which are then folded up and put in someone's hat or a similar vessel.

- Players take it in turns to pull a topic from the hat and then must speak on the subject for a minute without hesitation, deviation or repeating a word, with the exception of mentioning the given subject.

- Points are awarded when other players make a correct challenge for perceived hesitations, deviation or repetition. I'd suggest nominating a non-playing umpire to prevent arguments occurring.

# Dirty Doubles

### What's the game?

My friends Beth and John came up with this game on one particularly long and arduous journey. We were heading down to a festival on a Friday afternoon and got stuck in traffic as the sun beat down. The radio didn't work and the music selection was particularly dire, but we were blessed with a wide variety of audio books to entertain the children travelling with us. While the kids giggled their way through stories of wizards and wands, unbeknown to them we developed our own game that entertained us at a rather more base level.

### What do I need to play it?

An audio book. *Harry Potter*'s wand-laden tales are perfect.

### How many friends?

As many as are in the car.

### How do I play it?

- Get your audio book on and playing nice and loud for everyone to hear.
- The objective of the game is to spot the dirty double entendres that are unconsciously woven into the tale.
- Each successful spot scores a point.

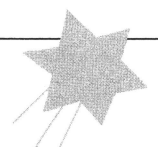

# Window Messages

### What's the game?

I can already hear the rumblings of complaint that will roll in from various quarters in response to this one. If you take it with a big fat pinch of salt, you'll see the amusement factor. This is for passengers only. Driver, keep your eyes on the road.

### What do I need to play it?

Plain paper and thick marker pens.

### How many friends?

Everyone in the car, excluding the driver.

### How do I play it?

- Everyone in the car decides on an appropriate and definitely not rude phrase that should be communicated to passengers in other vehicles. It might be 'Can I come in your car instead?' or 'Our car's better than yours'.

- Decide on a victim in another car who is not the driver, and everyone then has to guess what their response to the note is going to be, i.e. laugh, frown or stick their fingers up, for example.

- When you're ready, hold the note up to be seen by the non-driver in the other car.

- Whoever guesses the right response scores a point.

# Just Say No

## What's the game?

This game is about interrogation. I've always found car journeys to be a brilliant way to catch up with or properly quiz a friend, particularly on a subject they're uncomfortable talking about. It must be something to do with how easily eye contact is avoided as you stare out at the road, and there are always a wealth of opportunities such as, 'Ooh, shall we try the B1393 instead?' to tactically change the subject.

## What do I need to play it?

An inquisitive mind and some topics to cover.

## How many friends?

Everyone in the car.

## How do I play it?

- The rules are that players mustn't say 'Yes' or 'No' during one minute's intense interrogation. The only other rule is that they must always tell the truth.

- Players take it in turns to be the victim while everyone else around bombards them with questions to try to force them to say 'Yes' or 'No'. All questions must be answered, and there's a penalty of an additional ten seconds for a hesitation.

- If the victim makes it to the end of a minute without messing up, they get a point.

# NINE

# Sporting Organised Fun

*Ah: the sharp scent of sweat in the air; the note of testosterone as it pumps its way through the competitors' veins; a friend's normally jovial smile, hardened and replaced by the glare of a savage animal, intent on catching its prey.*

*Competition can change a person and an atmosphere. What started as a frolicsome day of fun can be transformed into a gladiatorial battleground within seconds. But it's not all bad; the suggestion of a chance to display prowess is also a fine way of rallying your friends to get involved. The normally too-cool-for-school chum can be rattled off their nonchalant chair to leap forward, fists gripped and roaring for battle to commence.*

# High-Heel Race

## What's the game?

The first time I came across a High-Heel Race was at the Transvestite Olympics on Sydney's Bondi Beach. Those elegant feline characters were competing in a balloon race and they fair pelted their way to the finishing line in pink patent stilettos with their balloons bouncing in front.

But it's not just the feisty Aussies who are partial to a stiletto stampede. High-Heel Racing is a prestigious and heavily sponsored annual event in Moscow, New York and Washington. Anyway, play at your ankle-twisting peril.

## What do I need to play it?

A fine pair of high heels per racer. You might have to go to a special cross-dressing shop to find a pair that fit the boys.

## How many friends?

As many as dare take part.

## How do I play it?

- Get the competitors lined up at the starting line with high heels firmly on their feet.
- On the word 'Go!', players race to the finishing line.

# Leapfrog Race

### What's the game?

I hadn't played leapfrog for years when I tried this one out last year at a friend's party in a local park. You may find that you've lost the natural flexibility of your youth, but don't let this put you off. With a little practice you'll be hurdling your friends with the best of them.

### What do I need to play it?

Just your good energetic selves.

### How many friends?

You need quite a few of you to make it a decent race. I'd suggest a minimum of two teams of five.

### How do I play it?

- Get the teams to each form a circle with about a metre between each other, and get everyone to bend over and place their hands on their knees.

- On the word 'Go!', the first person to go leapfrogs over the person in front of them and all around the circle. When they get back to where they started, they tap the person in front of them and they leapfrog around the circle too, and so on.

- First team to finish wins.

# Backseat-Driver Race

## What's the game?

This is a great test of someone's backseat-driving skills and their partner's tolerance of being directed. In this race, one half of a couple is blindfolded and guided on their stumbling dizzy way across the assault course and to the finishing line by their partner.

## What do I need to play it?

A blindfold per racing couple and some bits and bobs to create an obstacle course – upturned buckets or paint tins, sticks stuck in the ground to weave in and out of, a plank to balance across – whatever you can get your hands on.

## How many friends?

As many friends as want to play.

## How do I play it?

- Set up your assault course using the items you have gathered.
- Pair everyone up and get them to decide who's being blindfolded and who's driving, and get the former group to put the blindfold on and stand at the starting line.
- On the word 'Go!', drivers must spin their blindfolded partners five times and then let them head off. Drivers must shout instructions to their partners to navigate them through the course and to the finishing line.
- First pair back are the winners.

# Sack Race

## What's the game?

The sack race used to be a fixture at country fairs, village fêtes and school sports days across the country, but as Britain moves towards an American-style litigation culture, nuggets like this are starting to disappear. Make your protest heard by keeping the Sack Race alive before it falls victim to a fearsome health-and-safety culling.

The Sack Race is quite simply a race to the finishing line with your legs handicapped by being stuck in a sack. Traditionally, people used those old hessian potato sacks, but as they become harder to get hold of, you can conjure up a range of alternatives. Contestants may try all sorts of techniques, but the most effective is to make giant leaps with your feet close together.

## What do I need to play it?

One sack per racer. Alternatively those heavy-duty green garden waste bags also do the job, though you'll need to make sure contestants take their shoes off.

## How many friends?

As many as you can fit on your race course, plus someone to act as umpire.

## How do I play it?

- Get everyone lined up in their sacks at the start of the course.
- On the word 'Go!', racers need to bounce their way down the designated course, racing to be the first across the finishing line.

# Flowerpot Race

## What's the game?

This is harder to explain than it is to play. It's a race to the finishing line via two flowerpot stepping stones that you move forward on. Confused? Read on.

## What do I need to play it?

Two terracotta flowerpots per contestant; old paint tins are a great alternative. They need to be substantial and strong enough to stand on.

## How many friends?

Enough of you to make it a race.

## How do I play it?

- A starting and a finishing line are marked out. If you're particularly organised, you can mark a more elaborate course around the garden.

- Contestants turn their flowerpots upside down and then use them as stepping stones to race to the finishing line. Contestants begin by standing on one flowerpot behind the starting line. When the race begins, they each place their second flowerpots in front of them and step onto them, before moving their first flowerpot in front and stepping onto them, and so on.

- The first person to the finishing line wins. If you fall off or touch the ground at all, you have to go back to the beginning and start all over again.

# Hula-Hoop Relay

## What's the game?

The next game is an adaptation of the classic relay race but with the improvisation of a Hula Hoop being passed down the line. The art of playing with a hoop has engaged children for centuries. The whipping hoop was a cane hoop that children used to chase down the street with a stick. The 1950s saw a reinvention of the classic hoop by Wham-O-Toys, and in 1957 the world witnessed the birth of the Hula Hoop. This was the deciding game at our annual Organised Fun Olympics on Hampstead Heath one year. Who'd have thought that the humble Hula Hoop could cause so much tension?

## What do I need to play it?

A Hula Hoop.

## How many friends?

Enough for two teams, to make it a race.

## How do I play it?

- Get into two teams and spread out parallel to each other in two lines.
- The person at the top of the line starts by completing three successful spins of the hoop round their waist. They then pass the hoop down the line for the next person to do the same, and so on.
- First team to finish wins.

# Nose Ball

## What's the game?

A simple race in which competitors nose a ping-pong ball to the finishing line on their hands and knees.

## What do I need to play it?

One ping-pong ball per contestant.

## How many friends?

As many as want to take part.

## How do I play it?

- Get your contestants lined up at the starting line on their hands and knees with their noses to the ground and ping-pong balls in front.
- On the word 'Go!', contestants have to race to the finishing line nudging their ping-pong ball in front of them.
- First one across the line is the winner.

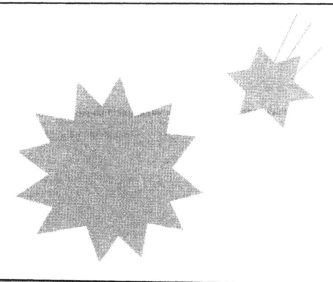

# Potato Race

## What's the game?

Another one that's highly amusing to watch. As contestants are blindfolded, you just need to make sure they don't get too eager with their potato-foraging and smack into each other.

## What do I need to play it?

A sack of potatoes and a blindfold and bucket per pair. You probably need around eight potatoes per player.

## How many friends?

Great for smaller groups, but you really need an even number. Four or six is perfect.

## How do I play it?

- First of all, set up your course by scattering the potatoes in front of the competitors.
- Next, get everyone to pair up and put a blindfold on one of each of the pairs.
- On the word 'Go!', the blindfolded players must race around to grab as many potatoes as they can while their partners shout out directions. When their arms are full, they race to the buckets and drop in their haul before carrying on again.
- Once all the potatoes are collected, the pair with the most in their bucket wins.

# Egg and Spoon Race

## What's the game?

This game does what it says on the tin: players each race to the finishing line with an egg balanced on a spoon.

## What do I need to play it?

An egg and spoon per player and a clear space to hold a race.

## How many friends?

As many as want to take part.

## How do I play it?

- Get the players lined up at the starting line with their eggs (boiled or not, depending on how much mess you want to make) balanced on their spoons.

- On the word 'Go!', contestants race to the finishing line. If their egg falls off the spoon, they must go back to the starting line and begin again.

- First across the line is the winner.

# Blindfolded Ankle Race

## What's the game?

This one's not for pregnant ladies or those with a tendency towards dizzy spells. A normal blindfolded race is made more complicated when contestants must hold their ankles as they race towards the finishing line.

## What do I need to play it?

A blindfold per player, and enough room to have a race.

## How many friends?

As many as you can rustle up to play.

## How do I play it?

- Get contestants blindfolded and lined up at the starting line, bent over so they're holding their ankles. Racers have the option to adopt a forward-facing or backward-facing approach.

- On the word 'Go!', contestants attempt to race towards where they think the finishing line is while holding onto their ankles. You'll need a judge to shout 'Stop!' when the first three are across the finishing line – and to redirect anyone who's heading for the garden pond.

- If holding your ankles is a bit too dizzying, you can change the format to a Blindfolded Backwards Running Race.

# Balloon Relay Race

## What's the game?

This game is great for indoors in a big room or outside in a sunny garden. Players form teams and race each other while flapping a newspaper at a balloon to make it go towards their teammate.

## What do I need to play it?

A balloon and newspaper per team.

## How many friends?

As many as want to play.

## How do I play it?

- Get contestants into teams. I'd recommend no more than six people in each. Split them up so that half are at one end of the track and half at the other.

- The first person in each team to race holds the newspaper and balloon in front of them. On the word 'Go!', they flap the newspaper to create a draught that drives the balloon towards their teammates on the other side. They must not hit the balloon with the newspaper. As balloons are full of air, they have a tendency to veer off course. It's harder than you might imagine it to be.

- As soon as they get their balloon to where their team member is standing at the other end of the track, the newspaper is handed over and the next person continues the race by driving the balloon back to the other end of the track.

- The first team to complete the course wins.

# Crab Scuttle Relay

### What's the game?
You know how crabs scuttle along the sand sideways? In this race, contestants must do exactly that.

### What do I need to play it?
Somewhere to race.

### How many friends?
Enough of you to make it a race.

### How do I play it?
- Get everyone to lie on their backs with their knees bent and hands and feet resting on the floor and get them to push themselves up to create the shape of a crab. Make sure they don't reach their arms over their heads and push up into a classic yoga crab shape, as this will put too much strain on their arms and backs.

- Get everyone positioned at the starting line in a sideways position. On the word 'Go', crabs scuttle to the finishing line.

# Wheelbarrow Relay

### What's the game?

Another village-fête classic.

### What do I need to play it?

Some strong friends who are up for a race.

### How many friends?

A big group of you who are old enough and strong enough to make this work.

### How do I play it?

- Mark out your racetrack. I'd suggest no more than seventy-five metres, otherwise you're going to break your contestants before your Olympic event is over.

- Put everyone into pairs and get them to argue over who's going to be the wheelbarrow.

- Once that's decided, get the pairs all lined up at the starting line with the runner holding their wheelbarrow's ankles so that they're walking along on their hands.

- On the word 'Go!', players race to the finishing line. First across the line wins.

# Water-Bucket Race

### What's the game?

This is an ideal game for a blazing summer's afternoon. Friends race to transfer the water from one bucket to another using only a cup.

### What do I need to play it?

Two buckets and a cup per person and somewhere to race.

### How many friends?

This is a race that works for small groups.

### How do I play it?

- Set your two buckets at a reasonable distance apart. On the word 'Go!', contestants have to transfer the water from one bucket to the other, one cup at a time, spilling as little as possible.

# Fancy-Dress Relay

## What's the game?

This is a very amusing race that uses clothes instead of a traditional relay baton.

## What do I need to play it?

You need a set of clothes for each team. Each set should feature similar items to prevent any unfair advantages.

## How many friends?

Great for large or small groups.

## How do I play it?

- Get the teams lined up at the starting line with a box of clothes in front of whoever is racing first.
- On the word 'Go!', the first contestant has to put on the whole outfit before racing to their team member at the end of the track. On arrival they must take the outfit off and pass the clothes to the next player, who puts them on as quickly as possible before racing back to the next player.
- First team to finish wins.

# TEN

# Organised Fun Office Olympics

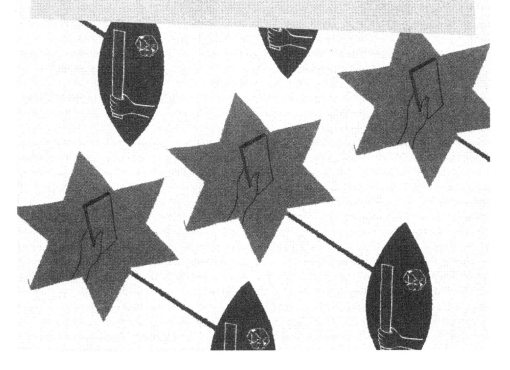

It's Friday afternoon at the office and, let's be honest, no one is really doing anything productive. It's that time of the week when you might be pretending to address those important tasks that have been swimming at the bottom of your to-do list for the past two months, but, come on, are you really going to do them? Instead, why not give up the pretence and issue an email bugle to your colleagues inviting them to join you in some Organised Fun Office Olympics.

To truly kick the games off in style, why not hold an opening-ceremony parade through the office. You could lead the way with a torch procession (an electric one will do the job) and perhaps persuade your boss to do an overly choreographed dance routine in the style of David Brent from the TV series The Office. Whatever your sporting disposition, the following chapter is stacked full of ideas to make sure the slow clock-ticking tedium of a Friday afternoon is a thing of the past.

# Office-Chair Jousting

## What's the game?

The popularity of the motorised vehicle has bought an end to our need for a noble steed, and as a result jousting is a dying sport, now only practised by eccentrics at festivals and country fairs. Do your part to help to keep this historical tradition alive and challenge your colleagues to an Office-Chair Jousting tournament.

## What do I need to play it?

An office chair and a broom per player. You also need to be fairly tough for this game, as it does involve being shoved off a moving chair. Usual safety warnings apply.

## How many friends?

Play is in pairs. You need a minimum of four to make it a match and as many as you can muster to make it a tournament.

## How do I play it?

- With broom held in hand, the riding player mounts their office chair so that the back of the seat is facing forwards. If your office chair has arm rests then sit on it in the normal fashion. The supporting partner meanwhile positions themselves behind the chair, ready to propel their partner forwards.

- Two sets of players then position themselves facing each other at a distance of ten metres.

- On the word 'Go!', the chairs are propelled towards each other with brooms held out in front. The object of the game is to dismount your opposing player by pushing them off using the brush part of the broom. This scores five points. You also score a point if you touch your opponent with the broom head. It is essential that the chair is kept moving throughout.

- Three attempts or 'charges' are allowed and scores are totted up. If playing a tournament-style event, the winner then takes on the next opponent.

# Wastepaper-Bin Long Jump

## What's the game?

Another game that comes with lots of warnings, as there is a high chance of breaking your legs, so play with caution.

## What do I need to play it?

Some willing workmates and a collection of wastepaper bins.

## How many friends?

As many as are daft enough to take part.

## How do I play it?

- The aim of this game is to be the contestant who jumps the furthest. Jumping distances are measured by the number of wastepaper bins you clear.
- Line three wastepaper bins up on the floor. Each contestant is challenged to jump over them. Once everyone has cleared them, another bin is added.
- The game plays on following a knockout format, with each person who clips a bin or fails to clear them being eliminated.
- The person who clears the most wastepaper bins is the winner.

# Synchronised Swivel-Chair Swimming

## What's the game?

The elegance and panache of the synchronised-swimming event makes it an Olympic classic every time. Recreate the beauty and grace of this scintillating sport for your colleagues to enjoy.

## What do I need to play it?

An office chair per contestant and some voting cards for the judges (i.e. ten cards numbered one to ten per judge).

## How many friends?

As many teams as you can muster to partake and a panel of judges.

## How do I play it?

- Now, this sport does require a spot of preparation. Get everyone into teams and give them a good thirty minutes (more if you have the time) to go away and work out their routines. Routines are performed using synchronised movement and dance while remaining mounted or seated on the office swivel chair.

- Once prepared, teams take it in turns to perform in front of the judges, who then mark each performance by holding up their chosen point card at the end.

- The team with the highest accumulated score wins.

# Office-Chair Obstacle Course

### What's the game?

This is quite simply a partner race to the finishing line involving weaving in and out of a line of wastepaper bins in your office chair.

### What do I need to play it?

An office chair and five wastepaper bins per competitor.

### How many friends?

As many as you can fit in. Play is in pairs.

### How do I play it?

- Line up as many lines of five wastepaper bins as you have competing pairs. You need to leave enough space between the bins and either side of racers to enable contestants to weave in and out, and prevent any dangerous collisions.

- Get the pairs lined up at the starting line with one person sat on the office chair and the other positioned behind, with hands on armrests ready to propel their partner forwards.

- On the word 'Go!', racers charge to the finishing line by weaving their office chairs in and out of the wastepaper bins. If a bin is knocked over, they have to go back to the starting line.

- First pair across the finishing line wins.

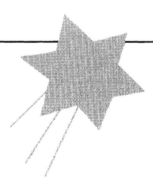

# Office Archery

## What's the game?

This game will appeal to the more sedate Olympian. The tournament involves catapulting rolled-up pieces of paper at designated targets.

## What do I need to play it?

An elastic band and a ruler per player, ten paper or plastic cups and a stash of paper from the recycling bin.

## How many friends?

As many colleagues as you can rally to get involved.

## How do I play it?

- First of all, prepare your ammunition by tearing and screwing up a pile of balls of paper and create your catapult using an elastic band and ruler. Next prepare your targets by clearly numbering the cups one to ten.

- Next, position your cups around the office. You might decide to balance one on top of someone's head, or if you fancy being a little less intrusive then position them on top of monitors and desks.

- Once set up, each player has ten shots. One point is scored for each ball that lands in the cup. The person who scores the most points wins.

# Pad Ping-Pong

### What's the game?

This is a game of Ping-Pong using your notepads and a ball of screwed-up paper.

### What do I need to play it?

Your notepads and a couple of sheets of used paper, screwed up or even taped into a tight ball, and a barrier to play over.

### How many friends?

Works best with two of you, with someone else acting as umpire. If there are more of you who want to play, then you can of course run it as a tournament-style event.

### How do I play it?

- Get set up so that you're each holding a pad and have your firmly screwed-up and taped ball of paper to hand. Position yourselves either side of a desk divided by a barrier, with enough room to move around.

- The rules are exactly the same as for a normal game of Ping-Pong, except that the ball cannot bounce.

- A point is awarded to the winner of each rally. Either opponent can score a point regardless of who served.

- The winner is the first to either fifteen or twenty-one points, depending on the length of game you want to play.

# Office-Chair Gymnastics

## What's the game?

Show off your gymnastic prowess by performing a routine on your office chair.

## What do I need to play it?

An office chair and score cards for the judges, ranging from one to ten.

## How many friends?

As many as want to partake, plus a panel of judges.

## How do I play it?

- Another one that comes with a safety warning: just don't get too carried away with showing off to your mates.

- In this event, players must demonstrate their ability to lift themselves out of their chairs using their armrests and perform a series of leg-based movements to impress the judges, for example holding them out straight, or perhaps some snippy scissor-like movements – you get the idea.

- Judges rate each performance, with the highest-scoring competitor winning the event.

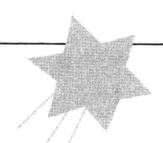

# Ruler Relay Race

### What's the game?

This one does what it says on the tin.

### What do I need to play it?

A ruler per team.

### How many friends?

As many teams as fancy taking part.

### How do I play it?

- Get contestants into teams of four. One member of each team is positioned at key points around the office, perhaps incorporating different floors or departments. Agree on a finishing line for the race.

- The first contestant to race holds the ruler in their hand and, on the word 'Go!', they sprint to the next person in the team. The ruler is passed on to each team member, with the final runner racing to the finish.

- First team across the finishing line wins.

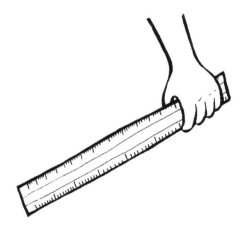

# Stationery Warfare

## What's the game?

For most of us, work can lead to boredom and irritation. We all have a couple of colleagues who manage to wind us up through their ability to push our buttons. It's an inevitable result of spending a vast percentage of our waking hours closeted in a small space with people we might otherwise not bother to say hello to. Stationery warfare is a great way to work through some of that frustration.

## What do I need to play it?

Ammunition and a firing device, namely screwed-up balls of paper and a ruler for each player. Use paper from your recycling bin rather than wasting new sheets. It's also good to have something to act as your trench or barrier to duck behind when in the throes of war.

## How many friends?

Between two and six people works best. It's good to have an impartial umpire who can keep scores.

## How do I play it?

- Get into your teams and arm yourselves with a ruler each and a good amount of screwed-up-paper ammunition and position yourselves behind your respective team barricades.
- The aim of the game is to make as many direct hits on the opposing team within a set time period. A direct hit is made by catapulting a screwed-up ball of paper at one of your opponents using your ruler and making contact.
- The team that makes the most number of hits wins.

# Work Dares

## What's the game?

For those looking for a considerable distraction, Work Dares can happily consume an entire week's worth of working hours. The aim of the game is to challenge your colleagues to a series of point-based dares to determine who's the bravest of you all. You'll need a degree of confidence in your job security, as, if taken too far, this one has the potential to turn sour. That's a gentle warning.

## What do I need to play it?

An agreed set of dares with a score sheet to monitor progress.

## How many friends?

A smaller group of two to four works best. You'll more than likely attract adverse attention, along with your P45, if you play on your own.

## How do I play it?

- First of all, you need to formulate a set of dares and agree how many points each one carries. For example, cartwheeling through your office shouting 'I'm so happy, I just can't stop myself' might attract two points, whereas breaking into a 'Thriller' routine in the middle of an important meeting should, I feel, qualify for at least five.

- I've featured a number of examples under the different point sections, but I'd suggest creating some bespoke ones for your work environment.

- One-point dares:
  - Reverse your chair around your desk or indeed the office as if you were reversing around the corner in your car. If anyone asks, just tell them you're practising for your advanced driving test.
  - Hop everywhere for two hours and if anyone asks what you're doing, say it's a yoga technique to strengthen muscles and improve balance.
- Two-point dares:
  - Roly-poly your way to the toilet or water-cooler.
  - Stand to attention, look straight ahead and bark 'Yes, sir!' every time someone asks you something. Do this with the first ten people who speak to you.
- Three-point dares:
  - Every time someone speaks to you, at the end of the conversation, look them in their eyes and say 'I do know, but don't worry, I'm not going to mention it to a soul'. Do this to the first ten people you meet.
  - Belch loudly every time anyone speaks to you, no matter who it is and follow it with profuse apologies that your gut is playing up.

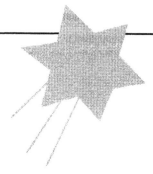

# Roller-Chair Rowing

## What's the game?

This one became popular after gaining huge viewing figures on Youtube. It's less of a game and more of a stunt, and should get even the grumpiest colleagues giggling behind their computer screens. It requires a bit of practice to nail the synchronicity, but the end result is well worth the effort.

## What do I need to play it?

An office chair on castors for each rower and something to make a cone-shaped loudspeaker out of.

## How many friends?

As many as want to play, but ideally a number that fits into a traditional rowing format, i.e. a two, four or eight with one person acting as your cox.

## How do I play it?

- Agree which rowing format you want to follow and position your chairs in a line one behind the other, with your cox seated opposite facing the direction in which you're rowing, loudspeaker in hand.

- Now, this takes a bit of practice, but you need to move in time with each other, so that as you reach forwards with your arms, you prepare to propel yourselves backwards simultaneously with your chairs. The cox must propel themselves forward in time with the rowers.

- Choose the most opportune moment to roll it out, and delight your colleagues by rowing your way through the office.

# DVD Discus

## What's the game?
Discus rules played with a DVD stolen from the stationery cupboard.

## What do I need to play it?
A DVD.

## How many friends?
As many as you can rally to play it.

## How do I play it?
- Define your throwing area by laying out a circle on the ground using a piece of string.
- Take your DVD discus and position yourself in your throwing area, ensuring that no one will be garrotted and that your throw will have the opportunity to reach its full potential. You can hold the DVD discus in any way and throw it using any technique. The only rules are that you must not leave the circle before the discus has touched the ground and you must not touch the ground outside the circle or the top of the circle rim with any part of the body after starting the throw.
- The furthest throw wins.

# List of Games

www.ingramcontent.com/pod-product-compliance
Ingram Content Group UK Ltd.
Pitfield, Milton Keynes, MK11 3LW, UK
UKHW040640280225
455688UK00002B/37